THE DESCENDANTS *of* GOD

CREATING A PROFOUND AWARENESS
OF WHO WE ARE IN CHRIST

BISHOP DALTON G. BURNETT

Copyright © 2021 Bishop Dalton G. Burnett

All rights reserved. No part of this book may be reproduced, stored, or transmitted by any means—whether auditory, graphic, mechanical, or electronic—without written permission of both publisher and author, except in the case of brief excerpts used in critical articles and reviews. Unauthorized reproduction of any part of this work is illegal and is punishable by law.

ISBN: 978-1-63950-075-8 (sc)
ISBN: 978-1-63950-076-5 (e)

Because of the dynamic nature of the Internet, any web addresses or links contained in this book may have changed since publication and may no longer be valid. The views expressed in this work are solely those of the author and do not necessarily reflect the views of the publisher, and the publisher hereby disclaims any responsibility for them.

Writers Apex

Gateway Towards Success

8063 MADISON AVE #1252
Indianapolis, IN 46227
+13176596889
www.writersapex.com

CONTENTS

Foreword v
Acknowledgements ix

Chapter 1   You are the Descendant of God 1
Chapter 2   You Carry His Love That Cannot Fail In You 42
Chapter 3   Lay Your Hands on the Sick and They Shall Recover ... 52
Chapter 4   You Carry His Blessing Upon You Right Now 69
Chapter 5   We Are Part of His Plan For These End Times 79
Chapter 6   Because We Are Sons 86
Chapter 7   What the Believer in Christ Is 96
Chapter 8   Miracle Mentality Miracle Attitude 113
Chapter 9   We Are Partakers of His Divine Nature 126
Chapter 10 Don't Sell Out Your Birthright Inheritance 136
Chapter 11 Looking Deeper Into Who We Are in Christ Jesus 153
Chapter 12 The Dominion Mandate has not Change it is
            Still in Force 170
Chapter 13 Shut it Down Like Jesus 185
Chapter 14 Confessions to Grow Your Faith Life Daily 189
Chapter 15 Scriptures that Show Us Who We Are in Christ Jesus ... 198

FOREWORD

Bishop Dalton George Burnett, a great man of faith certainly practices what he preaches. "**We are who God says we are and we can do what God says we can do**", a weekly confession along with the congregation he pastors each week. Bishop often says "the church must become problem solvers and as a **Descendant of God**", we have power within us to bring change. We all have the power on our tongues to command change.

Bishop is the shepherd of Harvestime Ministries and a man of passion for the things concerning God; reaching out into the community, teaching and inspiring others to overcome their challenges and limitations whilst striving to fulfil their highest possible purpose on this earth.

I met Bishop Burnett over 10 years ago and over the years I've had the pleasure of listening to this anointed man preach, teach and expound the Gospel of Jesus Christ.

I really experienced the TRUTH and POWER of Gods Word while in a meeting where Bishop ministered the Word. He took the time to go back to ***Genesis 1***. He began to explain that when God blessed us he gave us authority to operate in divine status just like Him after all he created us in His image and likeness. Bishop explained, that 'Whenever God wants something he speaks it out of Himself'. Just as God said, "**Let there be light**" and there was **light**, so it was! For me the penny suddenly dropped and there was an awakening and connection in my spirit to this truth. I believe that's when I begun to unlearn to relearn everything I was ever taught.

Bishop Burnett said he never envisaged writing a book but God opened his eyes to His Word and to that of the words that we speak daily. God continued pouring out His Word into his heart and now he shares this reading with you.

The Descendants of God is God's voice through Bishop Burnett. It is written in an uncomplicated way so readers understand. The author writes as himself, no frills or tradition he is simple, clear but effective. There is no way readers will miss what God is saying in this book for this season. It comes alive and unravels mysteries. Readers will not want to put this one down but read from cover to cover. You may find yourself reading **The Descendants of God** several times!

Having read this book myself I am convinced and believe that whatever I say from this point onwards is a **creative force.** In order to live **a successful and abundant life,** it depends on **the words I speak from my mouth**.

This book helps you to understand who you are, having the nature of God in you. It also explains that God **gave us all spiritual blessings from the beginning of time**. I am now enlightened to more truths in Genesis 1 than I ever imagined possible. You have the same creative force on your tongue given to you by your father that activates power just like Him. The very words that you speak could actually mean life or death. We are God's descendants and we are like Sons on the earth with God given authority. We have authority given to us and power on our tongues to command a thing and be established.

The Descendants of God makes it clear in order to rule and reign in Christ we must learn to only speak, confess and pray Gods word out daily. Only say what God says!

God has really used Bishop Burnett through this book to wake us up. I now know who I am in Christ and I'm persuaded to think and speak only that which is written in God's Word. It has changed my attitude which means my altitude will be great.

Those of you who read this book will begin to fully understand that you too are **Descendants of God and you already have the Kingdom of God in you**. You will learn about the Blessing of God and your capabilities, the power of positive confession and how to take your faith to a higher level and believe for those things you do not yet see.

There is no doubt that you will change the way you think, speak and start living. You will no longer see yourselves as others see you, but you will start seeing yourself as God sees you and believing what He has said. We are most definitely the Descendants of the Most High God!

You are being taken back into time (the Book of Genesis), to come forward again. You are blessed, stay blessed! The bible states, "know the truth and the truth will set you free." This book has been written specifically for you in mind. You will never be the same again, as you are brought into the full revelation knowledge of the Christ in you. You are who God says you are and you can do what God says you can do. The *Genesis 1* truth will set you free forever.

Through **REVELATION KNOWLEDGE**, Bishop now presents you with the most inspired reading for these end times. I believe there is about to be an explosion in the church. **This book** is an inspiration and example to us all. Rise therefore and shine **Descendants of God** for your light has come. I cannot wait for the next book.

Everyday do these things:

- *Speak God's words over your circumstances daily*
- *Speak God's wisdom into your heart daily*
- *Speak life to your self and others daily*
- *Be encouraged, you are victorious in Christ Jesus; you are who God says you are!*
- *Enjoy your reading, be inspired, and BE BLESSED!*

Foreword by Elder Lorna Clyne

ACKNOWLEDGEMENTS

This book **Descendants of God** has been birthed out of many years of pain, but in my pain God was there all the time to lead me in the right direction. I want to thank God foremost for my wife **Pastor Sandra** for her love, support, prayers and encouragement on this journey. Special blessings to our children, **Nigel, Sabrina and Sarah**, been there to help us when we needed them. I also want to thank my prayer team at Harvestime who have helped to birth this book. Thank you Elder Cline, Bishop John C Taylor, Bishop Dudley Bent, Bishop Canute Blake, Claudette, Marjorie, Audrey and all of you in my team that helped me with this book on who we are in Christ. We are the descendants of God and the devil can't change this truth. This is an unalterable principle of the Word of God. Ye are of God little children 1 John 4:4.

It is written acknowledge him in all thy ways and he shall direct thy paths.

I was struggling for years and wondered why there was not much flow of the anointing even though I took God at his Word and had much of the word in my heart. <u>What was lacking was the word missing out of my mouth consistently</u>. One day after much pain I came upon the writings of <u>Kenneth E. Hagin.</u> This showed me how vital it was to learn to walk by faith standing on the Word. I then started to pray for the sick but had no major break out of the healing power, then I came to the writings of **Kenneth and Gloria Copeland** also **Jerry Savelle.** Their teaching ministry changed my life forever. My connection to Kenneth in the Spirit is wonderful it has changed everything in my life. <u>**My days of being sick and broke are over.**</u>

I also started reading the writings of **Charles Capps** who taught me how to speak the word of God and keep speaking it no matter what we see. God also led me to the writings of **F.F.Bosworth and John G Lake**. I got Lakes sermons from Kenneth Copeland Ministries that changed me forever. In Pakistan I tested this and the fire fell, many people got saved and healed in my first crusade there in 2008. The first branch was established and there is now over 800 members and growing fast. They are on fire. I also came to the writings of **David Oyedepo** from Nigeria. By this time it was too late for the devil to stop me. Bishop **John A Francis** of **Ruach Ministries** also poured into me when I almost gave up because of opposition in the local church. I am forever grateful to him and his wife **Penny Francis. God used Penny to help me with just a few words**

One night I heard Pastor Penny said in London "**when God made us in heaven he did not put Impossible on us so who did**". I went from that meeting and continued my faith search to get answers from the Lord as to why his power was not flowing in the Local churches the way he wants it to. I found much of my answers in the writings and teachings of Dr Bill Winston. The problem was in our speech but we did not know it. Tradition is one of the greatest giants in the body of Christ that must die. These men as well as **Mathew Ashimolowo** of **KICC** were used by God to help me see my status in the kingdom of Jesus Christ Eph 1:3.

I came upon the writings of **John Osteen**; my God it helped me so much. Only in heaven he will know. Now as I daily apply the word, I can see the power of God flowing so easy in my life and in the local church. I want back all that Satan stole from me and my church and we are taking it all back in the name of Jesus Christ. **I have repeated certain things in this book very often in order to help the reader.**

If you want to see God work for you practice his word daily and he will step in and bring change to your life. God only work with his word.

Blessing of Abraham on you all as you read on.

Bishop Dalton G Burnett

CHAPTER 1

YOU ARE THE DESCENDANT OF GOD

Genesis 1:26 *And God said, Let us make man in our image, after our likeness: and let them have dominion over the fish of the sea, and over the fowl of the air, And over the cattle, and over all the earth, and over every creeping thing that creepeth upon the earth.*

This was the greatest announcement that God ever made in heaven. Here is the first revelation of God's great secret- the secret of the family of man inside of God. This is the first mention of mankind.

Man was to be an exact photo copy of the Almighty God capable of operating on the same level of faith as God. God is a faith God. So this was to be done, with God's word in the mouth of the man.

You notice that man was placed over all of God's, creation Gen 1:28. We were created inside of God first, and then God breathed the man into a clay/earth body Genesis 2.

The next verse is where we take our stand, as to who we are in Christ Jesus, and what is our authority on the earth.

Genesis 1:27 God created man in his own image, in the image of God created he him; male and female created he them.

And God blessed them, and God said unto them, Be fruit-full, multiply, replenish the earth, and subdue it and have dominion over the fish of the sea, and over the fowl of the air, and over every living thing that moveth upon the earth.

The first thing that ever happened to man was the impartation of the **Blessing** of the Lord into him and on him. Then fruitfulness, multiplication, Replenishing, subduing and dominion power was pronounced on man and in man. These are the first things man heard.

To replenish is to refill, fill, stock up, restock, reload, top up etc, therefore some thing was here before man got here. Our job is to bring good change where ever we are in this world. We do this with the blessing of the Lord on our lives. Genesis 1 is the greatest part in the whole bible. Everything that is happening in the world stems from Genesis 1. Satan hates the divine status that God gave to man in:

Genesis 1:28 And God blessed them, and God said unto them, 'Be fruit-full, and multiply, and replenish the earth, and subdue it: and have dominion over the fish of the sea, and over the fowl of the air, and over every living thing that moveth upon the earth.'

We are in a spiritual War that originated in the heavens

Be strong in the Lord and in the power of his might. Put on the whole armour of God for we wrestle not against flesh and blood but against evil spirits/powers and spiritual wickedness in high places **Eph 6:10-18, Isaiah 14**. The Lord God made man and put him on earth to represent him/ to rule/dominate the earth on his behalf. But man sold out on God in the Garden. We are involved in a spiritual war that started long before time began according to **Genesis 3:1** '*And I will put enmity between thee and the woman, and between thy seed and her seed; it shall bruise thy head, and thou shalt bruise his heel*'. Right at this point I want you to understand that God operates in the earth realms strictly by his Word. He does nothing here in the earth without speaking his word first to man. We are his ambassadors in the EARTH today.

Amos 3:7 *Surely the Lord God will do nothing, but he revealeth his secret unto his servants the prophets. The lion hath roared, who will not fear? the Lord God hath spoken, who can but prophesy?*

This is hard for religious people but it is bible truth and must be accepted if we are going to deal with the living God. In terms of his plan for how we must operate in this world. Man is a direct product of the word of the living God, <u>the descendant of God</u>, designed by God to represent Him on the earth. God's word in the mouth of man is the greatest force in the universe. The system is designed by God where He speaks and man repeats what he said on the earth, the result is miracle working power. *Luke 21:15 For I will give you a mouth and wisdom, which all your adversaries shall not be able to gainsay nor resist. Gen 1:28, Rom 10:9-10 9 That if thou shalt confess with thy mouth the Lord Jesus, and shalt believe in thine heart that God hath raised him from the dead, thou shalt be saved. For with the heart man believeth unto righteousness; and with the mouth confession is made unto salvation. Genesis 1:26, Numbers 14:28 Say unto them, 'As truly as I live, saith the Lord, as ye have spoken in mine ears, so will I do to you'.*

This teaching is about <u>who we are in God in Christ</u> by the Holy Spirit, *2 Cor 5:17 Therefore if any man be in Christ, he is a new creature: old things are passed away; behold, all things are become new.* We are setting forth by the word of God what we are in Christ, where we are in Christ and what we have in Christ. God's word is the most powerful force in the universe; if you have God's word you have it all. Adam was designed to live strictly by the Word of God, not by the word of the enemy Satan. You notice in Genesis 3 when the serpent approached the woman, his main concern was <u>'what God said'.</u> He questioned in *Genesis 3:1* "HATH GOD SAID". The devil is terrified of the word that comes out of the mouth of God and he is terrified of man speaking the word of God as a life style. <u>You are the descendant of the living God</u>. You are designed to speak after God himself.

The spiritual life force of God's eternal word propelled the earth and the universe into being, which are still upheld by <u>*"the word of his power".*</u> *Heb 1:1-2 God, who at sundry times and in divers manners spake in time past unto the fathers by the prophets, Hath in these last days spoken unto us by his Son, whom he hath appointed heir of all things, by whom also he made* *the worlds. You are the descendant of God. <u>You are of his word seed.</u> Being born again not of corruptible seed but of incorruptible seed by the word of God which liveth and abideth forever,* **1 Peter 1:23**. *The sperm that made you is the seed sperm of God's eternal word, so all of us that are born again are God's children. We are God's sons on the earth today.* **John 1:12** *But as many as received him, to them gave he power to become the sons of God, even to them that believe on his name,* **1 John 3:1-3** *Behold, what manner of love the Father hath bestowed upon us, that we should be called the sons of God: therefore the world knoweth us not, because it knew him not. Beloved, <u>now are we the sons of God</u>, and it doth not yet appear what we shall be: but we know that, when he shall appear, we shall be like him; for we shall see him as he is. And every man that hath this hope in him purifieth himself, even as he is pure. Now are we the sons of God.*

I want you to notice that nothing happened until **God spoke** what he had in his heart out of His mouth. He had to speak in order for it to happen. It was as He spoke, creation, took place. But what we tend to do, as God's people is to, forget that we are **supposed** to copy God. We are supposed to talk like Him, think like Him, and act like Him every day. Not just when things are alright but all the time as his representatives on the earth.

We are supposed to say what He has said in His word, and this is how we must live our lives on Earth. This is what it means to walk and live, by the faith of God, it means, we must only say what God has said about us. Every thing in Genesis 1 was as a result of the spoken word of God. He spoke them from the invisible into the visible. Light – life – vegetation – cattle – real estate, fish all came into being after God spoke them out of His heart and mouth. We need to learn to bring forth the right things out of our hearts into manifestation out of our mouth. '*A good man out of the good treasure of the heart brings forth good things: and an evil man out of the evil treasure brings forth evil things*', **Matt 12:35**.

You need to understand that, you are in the <u>image and likeness</u> of this great and awesome God, you are His image on the inside, you are in His likeness. You are internalised as a born again believer with His might, the core of God's being is in you now. You have His power and divine ability on the inside of you. *Jesus said "the works that I do, shall ye do also".* **John 14:12.** *Ye shall receive power* **Acts 1:8**.

You can do these new things because you are after His kind, and all things in the Earth realms have to obey your <u>voice of faith</u>. Jesus put it this way in **Mark 11:23** *'For verily I say unto you, That whosoever shall say unto this mountain, Be thou removed, and be thou cast into the sea; and shall not doubt in his heart, but shall believe that those things which he saith shall come to pass; he shall have whatsoever he saith'.* You shall have what you say! You need to get the revelation in your spirit that, there are spiritual principles that were here before you arrived on earth.

God's order has been in the Earth realms before you were born. The greatest forces are spiritual forces which made all natural forces. *You need to always remember that.* And the earth was without form, and void; and darkness was upon the face of the deep. And the Spirit of God moved upon the face of the waters. Genesis 1:2. Ye are of God, little children, *and have overcome them: because greater is he that is in you, than he that is in the world,* 1 John 4:4. So if the spiritual made the natural then the natural is subordinate to the invisible. All that we see with our natural eyes is not all there is to life on earth.

These forces are invisible but because they are of God, they are the creative forces that rule the universe. Satan is using spiritual forces that Adam gave him in the rebellion. Satan has no power over man except what Adam gave him or what we give him with the words of our mouth. This is why Paul said, *'give no place to the devil'* Ephesians 4:27 . It is a very clear revelation in the word of God that every man in this world shall have whatsoever he says and believes in his heart, Mark 11:23. This law will work all the time anywhere in the world.

Always remember you are what God says you are not what the world says. Your maker/designer/creator has the right to say what you are, and what your responsibilities are. You are in His image and likeness, His image in you gives you your identity, His likeness in you gives you your potential. You are His descendant.

You can live just like Him if you really want to. The secret of how to live like Him is revealed in the written word of God. **Matt 4:4** *But he answered and said, It is written, Man shall not live by bread alone, but by every word that proceedeth out of the mouth of God.* **John 7:23** *If a man on the sabbath day receive circumcision, that the law of Moses should not be broken; are ye angry at me, because I have made a man every whit whole on the sabbath day? God said, "let us make man in our own image and likeness* **Genesis 1:26.** *This was divine notice to all spiritual beings that man was to be like God, with the ability to wield authority, dominion and power.* <u>God said "let them rule"</u> *Genesis 1:26.*

Man was to be over all of God's creation. **Psalms 8:6** '*Thou madest him to have dominion over the works of thy hands; thou hast put all things under his feet*'. Man was to be the master of satan and all angelic beings. In Genesis 1:26-28 Man was a Son of God. All creation was pre-programmed to obey the voice of man in the earth. Satan was mad about this. <u>Stop thinking that the Lord is so high you can't get close to Him.</u> You are joined to him.

<u>It is the plan of God for man to be the family of God this was the plan all the time.</u> <u>The Lord was thinking about all of us before he made us. He had us secretly in the core of his being.</u> We are one with him **1 Corinthians 6:17** "*He that is joined unto the Lord is one spirit*". Think about that for a while.

You are what God says you are, whether you feel like it or not. Feelings have nothing to do with God's decision in His word about you. His decision in Christ has made you His blood covenant family Ephesians 2:19. What God has said about you in His word is the truth and we should not lie against the truth **James 3:14**. You must never voice out what the world says about you or what your feel. Voice out of your mouth only what God has said about you. This is the way you will get God to work for you because God will do exactly as you say. *"As I live saith the Lord as you have spoken in my ears that will I do unto you"* **Numbers 14:28**. You shall have what you say. *'For verily I say unto you, That whosoever shall say unto this mountain, Be thou removed, and be thou cast into the sea; and shall not doubt in his heart, but shall believe that those things which he saith shall come to pass; he shall have whatsoever he saith',* Mark 11:23.

This is the unchanging Law of faith that governs the invisible and, the visible world. What we do not yet see already exists in the realms of the invisible. Therefore, we take the word of faith which we receive from God and call things that are not as though they were into our natural realm Romans 4:17. This is one of God's principles that cannot change which has always been. This is how God set things up when he created the heavens and the earth and this is how man is designed to function. To function properly we must do as the Lord has said in His Word because it is the manual for our lives. This is a powerful principle; remember it is in force now. This can't change and the Word cannot be broken. *If he called them gods, unto whom the word of God came, and the scripture cannot be broken,* **John 10:35.**

Man was created out of the very core of God's being, nature and substance; man that is born again is the righteousness of God in the earth. Satan has no power or authority over man that is born again in Christ - none! **Luke 10:19** "Behold, I give unto you power to tread on serpents and scorpions, and over all the power of the enemy: and nothing shall by any means hurt you". There is no power in the hands of the devil that, as new creation people, we do not have authority over. We just need to learn to operate from our divine status in the Lord Jesus Christ. This was given to us in Christ before the world began.

Believers you are the voice of God on the earth today and Jesus is your voice in heaven. Jesus said; he that confess me before men him will I confess before my father in heaven. The more we speak the word on earth and confess Christ is the more he will do the same regarding us in Heaven Jesus said if we confess him on earth he will confess us in heaven before the angels. <u>God is totally committed to your voice on earth and the angels are activated by your voice on the earth.</u> ***Psalms 103:19, Num 14:28, Mark 11:23, Rom 10:9-10***, <u>God can't give you the new birth until you confess it out of your mouth.</u>

The voice of Adam was unlimited in the earth just like God's voice is unlimited in heaven. Adam was able to reign/rule/dominate/subdue all things in the earth with his voice. As a son of God in Christ Jesus you are a direct descendant of God. You have that same power in you to resurrect dead situations and re-arrange and to re-write your destiny. You can dictate your future by learning to speak just like God. This is why when Adam sinned God started to say what he wanted and Jesus came and accomplished God's spoken Word. Gen 3:15. You can operate just like Jesus if you start to do as the word says. (The word is God).

The blessing, endowment, power and dunamis of the Lord made Adam <u>fruit-full</u>. Adam was equipped and ordained with the blessing on Him all the time until he sinned. The only thing that can shut the blessing off the life of the believer is when we play with sin and do not repent. As a born again person you have this same blessing power inside of you now. **Acts 1:8** *'Ye shall receive power after the Holy Spirit is come upon you'*. The spirit upon you is the blessing upon you **Psalms 3:8** *"Thy blessing is upon thy people"*. Luke 10:19 "Behold I give you power over all the power of the enemy and nothing shall be any means hurt you".

The world cannot understand the blessing because the blessing does not operate by the systems or **principles of this world**; but by the word of God that is not of this world system. *God said, "my thoughts are not your thoughts and my ways are not your ways"* **Isaiah 55:8**. We cannot operate like the world and get miracles from God. We must learn to operate by the faith of his word.

Jesus gave us back his power and authority as His blood brothers on the earth. *'We over come satan by the blood of the lamb and by the word* *of our testimony',* **Revelation 12:11.** *Jesus said, 'as the Father hath sent me even so send I you', **John 20:21**.* His anointing is on us **1 John 2.** The true church is the body of the anointed one and his anointing; we are the ones who are recreated on the inside. The voice of the body of Christ has final authority in the earth. We are told that *'Whatsoever ye shall bind on earth, shall be bound in Heaven,* **Matthew 18:18.**That is a law of the spirit world but you have to know it is so all the time, and work it with your tongue. Jesus said "I will give you a mouth that all your adversaries will not be able to gainsay or resist"* **Luke 21:15**. This is the kind of power that you have in your mouth as a believer. Jesus left us here to cast out the devils and sickness which is our duty as the body of Christ. We are the ones that must now manifest the power of the Lord in the earth. You are the descendants of the living God. When we truly accept this by faith we will see a, new breed of believers on the earth taking our place John 14:12.

Adam's voice was final authority in the earth. Adam had God's authority as God's representative. Man is just as God is, because he is of God. *1 John 4:4 'Ye are of God little children and have overcome them, because greater is he that is in you than he that is in the world'.* God has given us the work of speaking His all powerful Word just like him. As we do this, he gives us miracles signs and wonders in abundance. We need to understand how powerful our voices are in the Earth. Jesus said we shall have what we say. <u>The miracle is in what we say.</u> Our mouth is over all things in this world. Gen 1:26. This principle works for all of us on Earth all the time, whether we know it or not it is a spiritual law that cannot change producing positive or negative outcomes. *Jesus Christ the same yesterday, and to day, and for ever. Heb 13:8.* **The word is Jesus himself personified.**

When you read or hear your bible practice understanding that it is the Lord God.

<u>God said "let us make man in our image and after our likeness"</u>, so God created man in his own image and likeness **Genesis 1:26-27**. You are

the descendant of God. You are the offspring of God, **Acts 17:29**. <u>**Descendant means offspring**, heir and inheritor. Whatever God is we are also, we are joint heirs with Christ Jesus, joined unto him are we 1 Corinthians 6:17, Romans 8:17. We are sons of God 1 John 3:2.study all</u>

Understand that you are made of the word of God so whatever the word is, this is what we are. You are as strong as God's word is on the inside 1 John 5:4, copying God's word in your mouth and heart. You can operate on the same level as God; we are not great it, it is the Word of God. The Word of God cannot change in our mouth. It is the Word of God's power that is great on your tongue right now Proverbs 18:21. Man shall eat good in this world by the <u>increase of his lips by the increase of his lips shall man's mouth be filled.</u> There is power on your tongue. If you talk like God says you should talk, if you talk like a son of God, you will see the power of the Lord working in your daily life. This will change the impossible situations of life. YOU are the descendant of God. **1 John 3:1-3** *"Beloved now are we the sons of God".*

As God spoke in Genesis 1:2 it came out of the invisible realms into the natural world. Nothing could come until he called them the way he wanted them. Genesis 1:26. You are in His image and likeness so you must operate the same way. Your purpose, destiny and position are not people's ideas but are the ideas of God. This is revealed in the word. **John 14:12** *"The works that I do shall ye do also".* This is your potential as a son/descendant of the living God.

God has a clear cut eternal plan for your life Ephesians 2:10, Jeremiah 29:11. The secret of success is to labour in the word until you discover who you are in Christ. Jesus said, *"You have not chosen me but I have chosen you and ordained you"*, **John 15:16**. *The believer is a part of God himself in Christ Jesus.* **1 Corinthians 6:17** *"He that is joined unto the Lord is one spirit";* this makes you a descendant of the Lord God. You now carry his very life in you as a son of the living God. God has supernaturally connected us back with himself through Christ.

You are his workmanship created in Christ Jesus Ephesians. 2:10. There is a path prepared for you before the world began. You are on a journey of discovery so enjoy yourself. Friend, remember to help others around you with the power of God that is in you and upon you all the time. **Wealth and riches is hidden in you Psalms** 112. 2 Cor 4:7 *"But we have this treasure in earthen vessels"*. As I've said the whole bible and all that is taking place in the world today is about our dominion **Genesis 1:26-28**. God has never changed his mind about His people and his plan for man's dominion is still in force today. *"I am the Lord, I change not"* Malachi 4. God's plan for your life on this earth will never change, you must know this. It is the enemy who planned for us to deviate from the plan of God. <u>The devil is a killer of purpose and destiny</u>. In the name of Jesus that will not happen to you.

The enemy came into the world to hurt, kill and destroy people but Jesus came *"that we might have life and, have it, more abundantly"* **John 10:10.** Jesus came into the world to '*destroy the works of the devil', **1 John 3:8***. This is your purpose as well as a descendant of God and Christ. God has given you His power and authority to get the job done. Yes you have the very same Holy Spirit in you that was, in Christ and upon Christ, so you can operate as a representative of the Kingdom of God. Your work is to represent Jesus Christ with the gospel to the world so miracle signs and wonders follow your life. *You men of Israel, hear these words; Jesus of Nazareth, a man approved of God among you by* **miracles and wonders** *and* **signs***, which God did by him in the midst of you, as ye yourselves also know,* **Acts 2:22**.

It is time for the body of Christ to wake up and destroy the works of the devil; people are dying and the Church is still mainly sleeping. God needs all believers to stand up and say like Isaiah "Lord, here am I sent me", **Isaiah 6:8**. What are you saying about the call of God on your life? You may be hearing the call of God for years. Why not take action today and fulfil your purpose and destiny. Obey the Lord.

<u>The Genesis purpose of God has never changed</u>

God cannot change and the Word of God, which is God, cannot change. *James explains that there is never a shadow of turning with God, James 1:17.* Moses explains that God's word is irreversible. Jesus said the scriptures cannot be broken, **John 10:35.** God's first purpose for man remains the same today as it was when God made man. Nothing going on in this world today has the ability to change the mind of God about man because man was created to be in the family of God. Man was made out of God. God is <u>full</u> of compassion. Compassion is the creator of man, which means man is the love being of the great father God. This is why Jesus came into the world to redeem us from the curse of the law **Galatians 3:13–14**.

When the enemy messed man up in the Garden of Eden the first thing that God did was to begin to speak of the seed of the woman. **Genesis 3:15**. In the face of what seems apparent defeat, then God began to speak the Word of victory to Man. The enemy was terrified as he knew that the seed of the woman would crush his head in time to come. This is why satan focused on killing most of the prophets because he was terrified of the anointed words that came out of the mouth of God in the Garden, regarding the coming Messiah. *And I will put enmity between thee and the woman, and between thy seed and her seed; it shall bruise thy head, and thou shalt bruise his heel. Genesis 3:15.*

God said the seed of the woman would crush the head of the serpent. Thank God Jesus crushed the enemy, rose from the dead. We rose with Jesus, because he was our substitute for death. His victory is our free gift from God. Ephesians 2:1-8.

St. Paul says we are more than conquerors through Christ, **Rom 8:32**. We are not in a natural fight, it is a spiritual battle and our weapons are spiritual. Never focus on what you see to win full spiritual warfare. The time has come to take all that Jesus bought back for us on the cross. Jesus bought the blessing back for all of us. He has redeemed us from the curse of the law. He has brought the blessing back to us. *Christ hath redeemed us from the curse of the law, being made a curse for us: for it is* *written, Cursed is every one that hangeth on a tree. That the blessing of Abraham might come on the Gentiles through Jesus Christ; that we might receive the promise of the Spirit through faith,* **Gal 3:13-14 Learn to know that you are fully redeemed.**

He has brought the empowerment back, we are now equipped with the blessing. He has brought the glory back to us so we can live in the presence of the father again. Through His blood it is as though we had never sinned. All this, is because of the blood of Jesus Christ. Therefore we have been given all now, at the expense of Christ Jesus.

All we need to do now is to enter into His rest of faith because it is already done it is already ours. The healing and prosperity is all ours. Thanks be unto God who gives us the victory through Jesus Christ our Lord *1 Cor 15:57, Prov 10:22*.

God took full responsibility for the redemption of man because man is in the image and likeness of the living God. Man is the offspring of God the descendant of the living God. So can you begin to see this now?

This is an awesome reality that you must understand by faith in the word of God whether you feel like it or not. <u>Christ dwells in your heart by faith</u> *Ephesians 3:17*. You are like God on the inside, you are important to him. <u>You are a spirit born of God sustained by God, understand this in your spirit. Ye are of God little children and have over come them *1 John 4:4*.</u> You are an eternal descendant of God.

If you are born of God it means you are in His likeness, we are just like him on the inside. You are after His kind. Remember the law of Genesis is that like begat like. You are a new creature that the world has never seen before you are not of the world you are of God. You are of God. You are of God.

Jesus is now at the right hand of God and so are you, for you are part of the body of Christ. The devil does not want us to know this. You need to meditate on this truth until light comes, but it will come if you stay with this day and night *Joshua 1:8*.

You are the descendants of the most High God. We are like him then so we have His potential in us. Yes you have His miracle ability in you. We can operate just like God, because; as he is so are we in this world. *1 John 4:17* Jesus operated as a man without the limitations of this world.

Jesus spoke the word of faith every time he spoke to the seen and the unseen

Nothing is impossible to the believer, Jesus said, "all things are possible to him that believeth". And "nothing shall be impossible unto you", nothing. Jesus was using the Law of faith *Genesis 1:26* and *Mark 11:23*. Luke 17:6 "It shall obey you". Study Rom 10:9-10. **Faith is a law of the invisible world that overrides any natural law.**

Jesus operated by faith all His life on Earth and always got astounding results. God expects His Church to operate like this now using our mouth in the Earth to activate His power. The tree obeyed Him. The wind obeyed Him and devils obeyed Him. All sickness obeyed Him as He used the law of faith in Genesis to get what he wanted. We can speak the same words because He said we can and we can do what He said we can do. The people around Jesus have never seen that kind of faith authority results.

<u>Eph 5:1 'Be imitators of God'.</u> <u>We can operate just like Jesus.</u> If this is true which it is. This means we are on the same level like the almighty Jesus. We should not fail to understand that we are the body of Christ on earth today. We have His mighty Spirit in us now to do the works of Jesus Christ. Jesus declared, *"greater works than these shall ye do"* *John 14:12*. *He that saith he abideth in him ought himself also to walk even as he walked 1 John 2:6.*

We can crush the enemy with the weapons of spiritual warfare *2 Corinthians 10:1-3*. We have the mighty name of Jesus to use against the enemy who comes to steal, kill and to destroy. We can shout with power that we are far from satanic oppression. We can use the blood of Jesus to shut the enemy down.

Man was created by God and given full God like responsibilities over the whole earth. Think about that for a moment *Genesis 1:28* and God blessed Adam and Eve and said be <u>fruit-full</u> and <u>multiply,</u> <u>replenish</u> and <u>subdue</u> the earth and have <u>dominion</u>. God commanded us to Rule. So don't blame God for the mess you are in.

God said <u>let them rule</u>. So we are to rule over everything in this world in the name of Jesus. How do we rule? We rule by using the word of God in our mouth.

Don't keep looking at what you see in this world, keep your eyes on the word; that's the mistake that Israel did in the wilderness. Say what God say about you no matter what you see before you **Numbers 14:1-13**. *And all the congregation lifted up their voice, and cried; and the people wept that night.*

² And all the children of Israel murmured against Moses and against Aaron: and the whole congregation said unto them, Would God that we had died in the land of Egypt! or would God we had died in this wilderness!

³ And wherefore hath the LORD brought us unto this land, to fall by the sword, that our wives and our children should be a prey? Was it not better for us to return into Egypt?

⁴ And they said one to another, Let us make a captain, and let us return into Egypt.

⁵ Then Moses and Aaron fell on their faces before all the assembly of the congregation of the children of Israel.

⁶ And Joshua the son of Nun, and Caleb the son of Jephunneh, which were of them that searched the land, rent their clothes:

⁷ And they spake unto all the company of the children of Israel, saying, The land, which we passed through to search it, is an exceeding good land.

⁸ If the LORD delight in us, then he will bring us into this land, and give it us; a land which floweth with milk and honey.

⁹ Only rebel not ye against the LORD, neither fear ye the people of the land; for they are bread for us: their defence is departed from them, and the LORD is with us: fear them not.

¹⁰ But all the congregation bade stone them with stones. And the glory of the LORD appeared in the tabernacle of the congregation before all the children of Israel.

¹¹ And the LORD said unto Moses, How long will this people provoke me? and how long will it be ere they believe me, for all the signs which I have shewed among them?

¹² I will smite them with the pestilence, and disinherit them, and will make of thee a greater nation and mightier than they.

¹³ And Moses said unto the LORD, Then the Egyptians shall hear it, (for thou broughtest up this people in thy might from among them ;) The people committed suicide by how they were talking. No

matter what storms you face. You face them with the all powerful Word of God in your mouth. Remember you are the descendants of the Most High God and you are made after His kind you can operate by faith just like him.

No limitations were placed by God upon the man Adam as long as he obeyed God. The Church must learn to rule over the Earth following the example of Jesus and the early Church.

There is no limit placed by God on believers. Take back all that satan and his cohorts stolen from us. This is our time to rise over all traditions and act like sons of God on the earth. The time has come to be bold and daring like Caleb and Joshua, **Numbers 14:1-13**. Jesus said, *"As thou has believed so be it done unto thee"*, **Matthew 8:13**.

The only thing that can break our connection is sin. Stay away from sin it is not worth it so don't do it. Man lost control of the earth when he sinned against God Genesis 3.

SIN

Solomon said, *"Sin is a reproach to any nation"*, **Proverbs 14:34**. You are an offspring of God so walk like one Acts 17, 1 Peter 1:23. Man empowered the enemy when he obeyed satan. Disobedience is a very dangerous thing it is worst than witchcraft. It degrades man to the lowest levels of life. Sin caused Adam stop living by the Word and started to live by his flesh. We need to understand that to abandon God's Word releases death upon us. When we leave the Word we empower the enemy to work against us. Only the word can keep death away from us. The Word of God is the highway to life it is the highway to success and the blessing of the father. Therefore, no matter what you are going through hold onto the Word of the living God. Hold fast your confession Heb. 4:14.

What are you suppose to hold fast to? 1 hold fast to your redemption in Christ, 2 hold fast to your absolute victory in Christ over satan and his forces, 3 hold fast to the reality of the greater one in you, 4 hold fast to the reality of your dominion mandate of Gen 1:28, 5 hold fast to the reality of the new birth, 6 hold fast to the reality of your riches in Christ and absolute power over money and financial circumstances, 7 hold fast to what God says about you in His word and no matter what kind of opposition or oppression that comes against you remember Jesus said you shall have what you say Mark 11:23.

Paul said we must walk worthy of this great calling of God on our lives. The world system has failed, it's not working and many people are dying. God is asking <u>who will go for him to the world with his word in their mouth</u> ***Isaiah 6:8.*** Will you go? Rise to the level of the God kind of Life and let us take the nations for Jesus Christ. As a descendant of the living God, His nature is in you. You are the seed of Abraham and you are blessed with faith <u>full</u> Abraham if you are born again, *And if ye be Christ's, then are ye Abraham's seed, and heirs according to the promise.* **Galatians 3:29**.

Genesis Chapter 1:1-31 is full of the light and the wisdom of God it is one of the most informative portions of the word of God. God is revealed as the creator of the heaven and the earth. All things in the chapter were made by the genius creative ability in the spoken word of God. God said let there be light and the light burst forth out of His inner most being. All things were created by the word of His mouth. Absolutely no help was given to him. He is the only one with the ability to bring order out of the chaos that the earth was in after the fall of Lucifer in which the universe was damaged during angelic warfare.

When God was ready he spoke out of himself to change the darkness that was upon the face of the earth. Things seen and things not seen invisible were, all created by the word of God at the dawning of time. *'For by him were all things created, that are in heaven, and that are in earth, visible and invisible, whether they be thrones, or dominions, or principalities, or powers: all things were created by him, and for him',* **Colossians 1:16**. By the time Adam came on the scene, on the sixth day; all things were already in place. God said that he wanted a Son. Finally God decided to create His son, so He made man to be in control of what He created. *'He made man in His image and likeness',* **Genesis 1:26.**

We are the descendants of the Most High God; we are like him in our spirit **Genesis 1:27**. We were created out of what God is; we are an expressed image of God. We are His offspring's, His sons, His family.

The New Testament speaks of the family in heaven and the family on earth. Remember who you are at all times. Remember what the Word says you are. *'You are of God little children and have overcome them, because greater is he that is in you than he that is in the world'*, **1 John 4:4**. Man that is born again is in the very image and likeness of God himself.

Get these truths into your spirit man and confess them daily

You carry these attributes of God in you on a daily basis they are in the recreated you:

You carry his love that cannot fail – John 3:16.
You carry his power to heal the sick – Matthew 16:15-18
You carry his joy - Nehemiah 8:10.
You carry his prosperity – Job 36:11.
You carry his faith – Hebrews 11.
You carry his blessing in you - Genesis 12:1-3.
You carry his divine life – 2 Peter 1:1-4.
You carry his good news - Mark 16:15-18.
You carry his wisdom - 1 Corinthians 1:30.
You carry his blood - Rev 12:11.
You carry his power - Luke 10:19.
You carry his wealth – Proverbs 10:22.
You carry his name – Mark 16:15-18

The time has come for you to awake out of sleep. Shine so that others begin to see him in you and turn to him for help. Potipher saw that the Lord was with Joseph. Saul saw that the Lord was with David. God's dominion mandate for mankind has not changed. Jesus reiterated it when he said <u>*behold I give you power over serpents and scorpions and over all the power of the enemy and nothing shall by any means hurt you Luke 10:19*</u>

The above scripture passage sounds like Genesis 1:28 to me. Dealing with Dominion be fruit-full, multiply, restock/replenishing the earth subdue (control), and have dominion. This shows that man should reign over the earth in the name of the Lord. I see you reigning now in Jesus name. You are the descendant of God.

MAN IN CHRIST IS A SON OF GOD HE IS A DESCENDANT OF GOD

2 Corinthians 5:17 "Therefore if any man be in Christ he is a new creation old things are passed away and behold all things are become new". According to the word of God if you are in Christ you are a new creature that did not exist before. You are brand new, your new life is in Christ in God, you are a descendant of the living God Himself, the old way of life is gone forever, you are no longer in the darkness realm, you are no longer in the failure realm, you are no longer in the sickness realm, you are no longer in the poverty realm, you are no longer in the lack realm, you are now in the realm of God. Which is your rightful realm in Christ Jesus. Where are you? You are inside of Christ inside of God at the right hand of God Eph. 2:1-6Y You are God's incorruptible seed on the earth this is what you are so don't let people label you. And stop looking at yourself in the natural and see yourself, as God sees you more than a conqueror in Christ Jesus Rom 8:37.

<u>You are in Christ. Your address is in Christ Rom 8:1-17,</u> your identity is in Christ your title is a son of God, an heir of God, a joint heir with Jesus Christ himself. Is Christ above the angels? So are you in Christ. Are the riches of Christ unlimited? His riches are yours. You have passed from death unto life in Christ St John 5:24. You are now the recipient of eternal life the very nature of God, the time has come for you to understand who you are in Christ and embrace it without any hesitation, it is time to declare who you are, as it is written in the word of God, you sprang out of God *<u>Acts 17:29 you are the offspring of God 1 John 4:4 ye are of God little children</u>* 1 Peter 1:23 Study.

You came out of God, you are accepted in the beloved Eph 1, Christ is your life Col 3:1-4 study. Christ is your power Luke 10:19, Christ is your strength Psalms 27:1, Christ is your unlimited source of wealth and riches Proverbs 10:22, Jesus Christ is your wisdom, righteousness sanctification and redemption 1 Corinthians 1:30. You are his and he is yours.

Learn to consistently say (about yourself) only what God says you are.

You are God's Garden on the earth; you are the temple of God on the earth 1 Corinthians 3:16. You are the dwelling place of God on the earth, you are the joy of the Lord on the earth, you are the miracle of God on the earth, in Christ this is what you are, you are God's refreshing on the earth, you are God's ambassador on the earth, you are God's city on the earth, don't let anyone talk you out of this because as you search the new testament you will discover this is what you are. Remember you are always what the word of God declares you are, you are born of God 1 John 4:4. You are God's incorruptible seed investment in the earth today 1 Pet 1:23.

This is what you will discover in the word of God as you study the word daily. Everything I have said is what God has revealed about you in His word above. This is the word of the Lord to you, you are the descendant of the living God so rise up and take your place in Christ, come out of spiritual immaturity and grow up in Christ Jesus, put yourself on a word-fest and you will grow and develop daily into who God says you are 1 Peter 1:23. It takes practice to understand but you will get there, if you continue in the word.

1 John 4:4 according to this scripture <u>ye are of God little children</u> the born again believer is apparently, the direct product of God almighty Himself in Christ. This is what we are, we have absolute authority and power, over the devil and his cohorts Luke 10:19. This is what satan doesn't want you to know as a believer, he wants to rule over your life with fear, whereas God wants to rule over your life with faith and love. Satan uses care-filled words, sickness filled words, poverty filled words, destruction filled words, lack filled words and pain filled words, and debt filled words to rule over people. On the other hand God uses love filled words, faith filled words, prosperity filled words, and joy filled words, success-filled words to help His people. This is why we have to choose who we will serve the word of God or satan. God does not want us to halt between two opinions, we must decide, God or the devil. You

choose God by choosing to obey his word. I have decided to choose the word of God what about you? *You shall have what you say, Mark 11:23, 2 Corinthians 4:7. But we have this treasure in earthen vessels.*

Your spirit is full of the unlimited treasures of Christ. Your spirit is just like God on the inside, you carry spiritual forces within your spirit. The faith of God is within you, your spirit is now immortal from the day you were born again. I know this is hard to handle but this is what we are in Christ Jesus. We are eternal beings the body is just a temporary house we live in. God now lives in us as eternal temples. *Christ the hope of glory is living in you Col 1:27 He will never leave you nor forsake you as He has promised in His word Heb 13: 8.*

1 John 3:1 always remember night and day that you are born of the spirit of God, and that which is born of the spirit is spirit John 3:1-7, you are not trying to be spirit you are a spirit born of God and your authority in the earth is the blessing. No man can operate in the earth successfully to please God without the blessing. So it is the blessing that gives us power over the enemy. The blessing of the Lord makes you rich and addeth no sorrow Prov 10:22.

Understanding your place of power, authority and privileges in Christ is vital to fulfilling purpose and destiny in Christ Jesus. You are like Adam before he sinned, in your spirit man. You are the body of Jesus Christ in the earth. You are an eternal spirit born of the most high. You are his child you are his offspring, that's what you are whether you feel like it or not, that's what you are Rom 8:1. *You cannot fulfil purpose until you know who you are in Christ Jesus.* Gal 4:1. This is why we all need to grow up in Christ, and be fully matured up in his word of faith.

You are spirit of His Spirit; you are divine because He is divine. You are a partaker of his divine nature. You are righteous, because He is righteous. You are a branch of the divine vine. You are the fruit bearing part of Christ. His Zoë life, His nature, His being, His substance. All these unlimited spiritual forces are within your spirit as a new creation being.

His righteousness is in you. Because you are His, in spirit you carry His glory on the inside of you. You carry His anointing in you and on you. You carry on the inside the potential of Jesus Christ because you have His spirit, you have His power (Dunamis) internalised into you, when you got born again. John 1:12 "as many as receive Him to them gave he power to become the sons of God". This is you he is talking to you. <u>Learn to personally apply the word of God to yourself daily</u>. Jesus said, *<u>greater works than these shall ye do John 14:12</u>*

You are of the super race that has power over all the power of the enemy Luke 10:19. Jesus is the head of God's **new super race of men**. God achieved this on the day of Pentecost through Jesus. You cannot be defeated because you have already won in Christ. Romans 8:1-17.

All that the enemy is trying to hold back from you is already yours. Jesus paid for your new birth and all the honours and rights of the blood covenant that comes with it. Ephesians 1:7. You have redemption in Christ Jesus. His BLOOD is now yours; all the power in His blood now belongs to you. His blood speaks better things for you. You are a wonder to the world and to the angels. You are a sign to the world. All things are now possible because you know who you are in Him. The enemy is afraid of you and what you have on the inside – you can now STOP him dead in his tracks. You now have power and authority over him and all his devils Luke 10:19. Actually the power that you have is far superior to what the devil have. Acts 1:8 *<u>"But you shall receive power after the Holy Ghost is come upon you". Thy Blessing is on thy people Psalms 3:8.</u>*

You are unstoppable, Mark 16:17 because you belong to the God kind of beings, the God – kind of race *<u>Acts 17:29 we are the offspring of God</u>*. As He is so are we in this world 1 John 4:17. You are his heir, his offspring, his inheritor, his child, his son on the inside 1.John 4:4

I see you crushing the enemy under your feet in Jesus mighty name. I see your days of stagnation coming to an end, in Jesus mighty name. I bind the strongman operating against you in the name of the Lord Jesus

Christ. Everything that satan has programme against you into the sun, moon and stars I destroy it now in the name of Jesus Christ of Nazareth. The sun shall not smite you by day or the moon by night. Everything was created to be a blessing to you. God consistently desires that take up your position given to you by him. Jesus said, <u>it is the fathers good pleasure to give us the kingdom Luke 12:32</u>

I see you operating in the fullness of the blessing of the gospel of Jesus Christ. Hear me my friend, most of us attend Church, pray, sing and read the bible but we have not yet fully accepted who we are in Christ. Yet, this is the secret of divine success on the earth. We have embraced the tradition of man rather than embracing the word of truth. The word of God is the truth things in this world is a truth but God's word is the truth. However for us to see God at work in us and through us, we must learn to take God at his word. You see faith is only activated when we act upon the word, regardless of our circumstances Hebrews 11:6.

If we are the sons of God then we must have His awesome potential on the inside. This is why Jesus said, out of our belly shall flow rivers of living water. The time has come to go back to the principles of Genesis 1, where God showed us how to get things done by speaking them out of our hearts. We get out of our hearts what we put in it. We get out of the ground of our inner man what we invest in it. <u>This is LAW of the spirit world</u>. You put things in your heart by meditation in the word and speaking them. Proverbs 23:7.

Solomon said "<u>Keep thine heart with all diligence</u>, <u>for out of it springs the issues of life Prov 4:23</u> The way God has designed you if you study the word, you will find that we are able to plant the seed of the word of the Lord in our hearts and our spirit will work night and day searching the avenues of God to bring to pass what we have planted in our hearts. You notice I have said what we have planted, if you plant God's word the word of God will become what you say, that is what your spirit will grow because that's how your spirit is designed to function, it grows what you put into it. So be careful what you listen to.

Therefore, the same principle applies with the words of the devil, which are always negative words, which are always anti-covenant words, which are words of fear. The devil is full of fear so full your heart with the faith of God's word. This is why Jesus said we are justified or condemned by our own words Matt 12:34-35. You are designed as a descendant of God so that your life will follow your mouth. I want to say that again, your life will follow your mouth every day in every way. Your future is in your mouth, what you have today is what you have been saying for years, therefore, if you don't like what you see today you can change what you are saying and therefore change your future. This is how you are designed, you are a word spirit created by the God of words, everything about your life is words, everything about satan is negative words, everything about your financial problems, sickness or circumstance is words. <u>This world is a word planet</u>.

As Bishop Canute Blake in Toronto said to me we live in a <u>"word activated system"</u>, I have never been able to forget those few words. Most of us in the Church still don't understand that this is how we function either on the faith side or on the fear side, either on the light side or the darkness side, either on the hell side or on the heaven side, either on the Kingdom of God side or on the kingdom of the devil side. There is no middle ground; you shall have what you say. As a descendant of God you must remember this and control your tongue with the power of the Holy Ghost, always remember your spirit is connected to your tongue, your tongue is connected to the spirit world. You become a terror to satan and his cohorts when you put the word of God on your tongue and prophesy them over your life. This is how God's system works all the time. This will never change and it has always been so. Learn to become conscious of the invisible world that is around you your spirit, your inner man, the real you is a part of that world. Many people have forgotten the mother world that created the natural.

Be very careful of so call prophets who totally disregard the scriptures, they have no time for the written word but the only thing in this world that cannot be broken is the <u>scriptures, God's language. Jesus said the Scriptures cannot be broken</u> In John 10:35.

Jesus prophesied the scriptures over His own life; it is the wisdom of God revealed in scripture that man is designed to speak what God says in faith. We must do this very often several times a day and night, as we do this effectively, we are releasing Kingdom of Heaven spiritual forces, to work on our behalf to bring us into purpose and divine destiny. That was planned for us from the foundation of the world. You are the descendant of God, you are what God says you are, you are where God says you are in heavenly places in Christ Jesus. You are design to function just like Jesus Christ with His word in your mouth so don't, be afraid, because you are what God says you are. What God said is taking place out of your view in the invisible realms where God is, in your spirit, around you, over you and under you. You can't see it yet but it is working, therefore keep speaking his word over your life day and night.

You are designed by God to get only what you speak out of your mouth. Your life will be filled with the increase of your lips. You intimidate the devil with the words of your mouth Luke 21:15. When you speak the word and believe it, the devil can't turn it. Nobody can stop you except you. God's language in your mouth makes you a winner all the time.

Three million Jews could not stop two men in the wilderness because they said what God said about themselves, they knew that God could not fail them. They knew that some how God would show up and bring His promise of the promise land to pass. I say to you today no matter what you see, God will show up for you, you will never let you down so, speak on.

You need to reach the place of knowing that God is on your side and no matter what he will take you over Joshua 1. "Be strong and of good courage" says the Lord, <u>I'll take you over.</u>

You are God's investment to your generation you are special because He is special, He is King and he has made you king on earth. The power is within your born again recreated spirit man so you can make it despite the lies of the enemy. You will make it. As a son the joy of the Lord is your strength. I cannot understand how some Christians have no joy. Something is wrong that's all I will say about that. If you want joy see yourself with it and speak it.

Man in Christ can operate just as how God did in Genesis 1. I see you rising up and taking charge of your divine status in Christ Jesus. I see you stepping into dumfounding breakthroughs in all areas of your life, things is about to change big time in your life. Your stagnation is over in the name of Jesus. Take your place in the Kingdom and do great exploits for the Glory of God Isaiah 54:17 "No weapon formed against thee shall prosper". *Daniel 11:32 "The people that do know their God shall be strong and do exploits.*

Sons of God carry the keys of the Kingdom, the key is already in your hands, rise up by the faith of God and use the Kingdom principle keys that you have been given. Rise like Joshua and smite your enemy in the spirit world with the weapons of spiritual warfare. Rise up and bind the strongman that has been hindering your progress. Bind him now in the name of Jesus. *Matthew 18:18 "whatever you bind on earth shall be bound in heaven, whatsoever you loose on earth shall be loose in heaven".*

Ephesians 1:7 in whom we have redemption through His blood even the forgiveness of sins. Man in Christ is a man restored back to dominion and put back into the garden of the Kingdom of God. Just as if sin had never been, we are back again redeemed out of the hand of the cruel enemy that has no mercy. By the grace of God we are back in the family of the Most High God. We have the garden back in the new birth, we reside in the Kingdom of Christ. We are under the protection of the blood of Jesus. In Christ we are delivered from the power of darkness, the blessing is back with a vengeance against the enemy.

The devil no longer has any right to hold us captive because man in Christ is under the umbrella of the BLESSING; Genesis 1:28, Genesis

12:2-3, Genesis 9:7. We are the redeemed, we are the blessed of the LORD Eph 1:3 "blessed be the God and Father of our Lord Jesus Christ who have blessed us with all spiritual blessings in heavenly places in Chris Jesus".

Paul told young Timothy to meditate upon these things so that his profiting could appear. Meditate upon these things, give thyself wholly to them that thy profiting may appear to all, 1 Timothy 4:15 Paul said "consider what I say and the Lord give the understanding in all things".

The Holy Spirit said in Proverbs 4 "in all thy getting get understanding". Because we do not meditate on these things we fail to grasp the reality of who we are and what truly belongs to us in Gods, plan of redemption. See yourself redeemed by the blood of Jesus in the name of Jesus and walk in the light of who and what you are in Christ.

The bible states that we are sons of God now, not only in the sweet by and by but now while we are in this world. Remember that Jesus is the Son of God and he was in this world, born into this world. The new birth in Christ gives us divine status in Christ Jesus. For God so loved the world that he gave his only begotten son that whosoever believeth on him should not perish but shall have everlasting life. Everlasting life being the nature being and substance of the living God St John 3:16.

Jesus did not come to hurt man but to restore man back to his Genesis 1:28 position with God. He humbled himself even unto death to make sure we could get back what is truly ours before the foundation of the world. Ephesians 2:10 explains that we are the workmanship of God of ordained by God to do good before time began. Solomon said "_that which hath been is now_". What God had planned before the world began found there fulfilment in the man called Jesus Christ, the anointed one and His anointing. The head of the enemy was crushed 2000 years ago so that God could get us back into his family. We are back in the realms of God we are back in the light realms this is where we are. We are His and He is ours.

We are one in Christ Jesus. **"He that is joined unto the Lord is one spirit"** *1 Corinthians* 6:17. As believers we are the blood brothers of Jesus Christ the son of the living God. All the rights and privileges are given to us in Christ Jesus in the promises of God. This is what ministers have failed to teach the Church and the purpose of the five fold ministry is to teach the Church these things so that the body of Christ can come into full maturity. Paul said *"till we all come into the unity of the faith and the measure of the stature of the fullness of Christ*. God wants us to operate as the body of Christ in the fullness of the gospel of Christ. Yes in the fullness of the blessing of Christ Jesus.

However, this will not fully happen until we recognise who we are as literal sons of God in Christ Jesus having Christ the hope of glory inside of us Colossians 1:27. We are the descendants of the Most High God. Offspring of God, sent by God to bring radical change to humanity, with the gospel of Jesus Christ. We are the body of Jesus Christ the son of the living God. We are the light of the world, because we are the children of light, we are in Him and He is in us. What a mighty God we serve. I see this revelation producing powerful miracles in your life in the name of Jesus Christ.

And because ye are sons, God hath sent forth the Spirit of His Son into your hearts, crying, Abba, Father. Therefore thou art no more a servant, but a son and if a son, then an heir of God through Christ Galatians 4:5-7.

When I first came upon Galatians 4:6-7, I was shocked. Friends, the only reason why you have been given the Holy Spirit is because you are a son of God now. This has nothing to do with how we feel at times. By the word of God we are sons now in Christ.

'Because we are sons' what a word!

Because we are sons God hath – (past tense) sent forth the spirit of His son into our hearts crying Abba father Galatians 4:5-6. Your heart is your spirit. Your heart is you. Your heart is the real you, you are an eternal spirit.

You are a spirit with the Holy Spirit within. Your spirit is far superior to your soul. Your body has a soul but you are first a spirit in the image and likeness of

God himself. The revelation is very important to getting to know the Lord's will. Because we are sons, is the reason God is working all things out for our good.

God will not allow His family to perish, He has invested himself into His family, and we are His eternal seed inheritance. We are His portion forever. David also said "the Lord is my portion". We are the people of God, a peculiar people. Nothing is impossible with the people, the sons of the living God.

The bible says that "the people that do know their God shall be strong and do great exploits. Man in Christ is never left on His own. God told him "I will never leave thee nor forsake thee. God said "I will not fail thee, so be strong and of good courage".

Mark 16:15-20 is about man taking his place of dominion in the Kingdom of the living God. It is about Genesis 1:26, Mark 16:15-20 and Genesis 1:28 these scriptures are really saying the same things regarding our divine status in the kingdom of God.

<u>"And God blessed them, and God said unto them, be fruit-ful, and multiply, and replenish the earth, and subdue it: and have dominion over the fish of the sea and over the fowl of the air, and over every living thing that moveth upon the earth" Genesis 1:28.</u>

And he said unto them, "Go ye into the entire world and preach/declare/proclaim the gospel (good news) to every creature. He that believeth and is baptised shall be saved; but he that believeth not shall be damned. And these signs shall follow them that believe; In my name shall they cast out devils;

they shall speak with new tongues; they shall take up serpents; and if they drink any deadly thing, it shall not hurt them; they shall lay hands on the sick, and they shall recover". So then after the Lord had spoken unto them, he was received up into heaven, and sat on the right hand of God. And they went forth, and preached every where the Lord working with them, and confirming the word with signs following Mark 16:15-20.

These words give us details as to what we are and how we are to operate in this world. The enemy has been working hard to get our focus off the divine mandate that the Lord has given to us. I see you operating in the mighty name of Jesus on a daily basis. Your time of obscurity is over. You will excel in the name of Jesus. You are a winner; you are made of the word. The word is the winner and so are you in this word. You are supernatural because you have the spirit of God living inside of you forever, you will never, never be separated from the Lord again. He is your father you are His child.

YOU ARE A SPIRIT DON'T EVER FORGET THIS

The spirit of man is the candle/floodlight of the Lord searching all the inwards parts of the belly Proverbs 20:27, 1 Thes 5:23 "You are a spirit with a <u>soul</u> and a <u>body</u>".

Friends get this into your spirit, once and for all. You are a spirit being just like God, you are a God like being. Divine power, divine potential are hidden within you right now.

God has hidden stuff in you that can cause you to be an asset to your generation. You were born into the world at the right time; you are at the right place for a miracle Job 32:8 "but there is a spirit in man and the inspiration of the Almighty giveth understanding".

Mediate on the word and until you get the right attitude. God's word when mediated on will produce miracle mentality in us. We are first of all spirit. It is with your spirit that you touch God with your faith.

We having the same spirit of faith, according as it is written, I believed, and therefore have I spoken; we also believe, and therefore speak 2 Corinthians 4:13.

Your body can't touch God only your spirit of faith. God has given you faith in your heart and in His word so that you can get back in touch with Him at anytime Rom 12:3, Ephesians 2:8.

Because you are spirit born of the spirit of God it is impossible to know yourself without knowing God, without having a relationship with Him. It is as we get to know Him in our spirit we find fulfilment, satisfaction, destiny, purpose and the reason for living.

Purpose and destiny will come alive as we spend time fellowshipping with the Lord in our spirit and in the word. There is no greater blessing in this life than having God in the spirit of man. Knowing He is your father. It is the greatest union in the universe. Nothing is more important to God than this. This is what Adam lost in the Garden. He lost the indwelling presence of the Lord that was in him. He lost the glory of God that was inherent within. He lost the abilities and attributes of God that was within him. He lost the righteousness of God that was in him. He lost the peace of God. The glory was gone when he sinned; wisdom abandoned him, but God's grace and mercy didn't. God began to speak about the seed of the woman that would bruise the head of the serpent Genesis 3:15. Jesus Christ came and won us back into the kingdom of God Gal 3:13, St John 3:16 study these scriptures.

You are in His image and likeness. You are a spirit. You are not in a natural battle, but an invisible spiritual war. <u>Satan is your real constant enemy</u>. There is a battle raging over your life on earth in terms of how you should live it. God wants you to live it His way. Satan wants you to live it his way. Because you are a spirit then the problems you face in this life must be spiritual. Most times in life we need to get our eyes off the natural and look by faith to God who is our father. <u>*For we walk*</u>

by faith not by sight 2 Corinthians 5:7. **You are the descendant of God.** The time has come to become fully conscious of who you are in Christ.

The devil wants us to stay ignorant of the spiritual things that rightfully belongs to us, he does not want us to know our potential or who we really are in Christ Jesus, Hosea 4:6. 1 Corinthians 2 "We have received the spirit of God so that we may know what is given to us". My people are destroyed for lack of knowledge. Lack of knowledge is a killer. All of us need to be growing in the things of the spirit. Your spirit has the ability to grow up in the things of God Just as how your natural body grows Ephesians 4 study.

The time has come for radical change in how we see ourselves. We must learn to embrace what God says about us, not what people or the world is saying. What God says is eternal reality. What God says is the truth. What God says is the answer. Learn to see yourself in Christ. Take your eyes off the things that are seen and focus on the unseen things of the spirit Col 3:1-3. How do you do this? By focusing on the promises of God.

"If ye then be risen with Christ, seek those things which are above where Christ sitteth on the right hand of God" Colossians 3:1.

You are a spirit so focus on the eternal things of the spirit. To be carnally minded is death. To think like the world is death. Study Rom 8. To think like God is life and peace in the Holy Ghost. Everything that the devil is involved in leads, to death and destruction. Everything God is leads to life eternal. God brings life, the devil brings death. Jesus said, *"I am the come that they might have life and have it more abundantly" John 10:10. This life is what your spirit man is made up of. Your spirit is full of the ability of God, if you are born again, so when you speak learn to believe what you say, and God will bring it to pass Prov 21:20.*

The spirit of man is the candle of the Lord Proverbs 20:27. This means that whatever God is going to do through you, will be done in your spirit and through your spirit man. Remember that the greater one who is the Holy Spirit is constantly living in you. You are always anointed because He lives within you. **Be God inside minded** and the miraculous will become normal for your. You are not a body you are a spirit with the life of God in you. You are over the devil not under him. You have the power to crush him under your feet Luke 10:19.*The Bible also said, the God of peace shall bruise Satan under your feet.*

There is a spirit in man and the inspiration of the almighty gives understanding Job 32:8. All the fruits of the spirit come out of your spirit that is where the power is. All the gifts of the spirit flow from the recreated spirit of the new creature. You are the duplicate of God in His image and likeness, you are a spirit being. You are a spirit being without any condemnation in Christ Jesus Romans 8:1. God himself has birth you out of himself for such a time as this. You are not an accident, God made you out of Himself with his word. There is purpose and destiny hidden within you by the Lord. God loves you because you are a part of Him. He will never leave you or forsake you. Always remember that you are a partaker of God's divine nature. When you were born again (recreation, you were recreated) with the special life of God in you. It is called ZOE the very life of God.

The devil does not want you to know this. God said be fruit-full, multiply, replenish, subdue and have dominion Gen 1:28. Please understand that God said these things after he empowered us with 'the Blessing'. The bible says, "And God blessed them", words were spoken over us by God from Genesis and God has never changed His mind about His plan and purpose for our lives upon the earth.

Release the fruitfulness that is in you by mediation in the word. Meditation will produce revelation and revelation will produce motivation. Motivation will produce action. Action on the word will produce results. Remember *Jeremiah 7:23, "Obey my voice and I will be your God"*

A SPECIAL RACE OF SPIRIT BEINGS

Friends you are a part of God's special race of divine family Deuteronomy 7:1-8. You have been given divine status in the new birth and by the rights of the blood covenant. The word says you are a partaker at the Lord's Table. You have arrived because God is your Father, your power, your ability. There is no longer any restraint 1 Samuel 14:6. All things are now possible because God is on your side Romans 8:32. *"If God be for us who can be against us?"*

On the inside God has made you more than a conqueror just like Jesus Rom 8:37 "In all these things we are more than conquerors". You have the power to multiply, replenish and subdue. You have dominion. This is not for 'in the sweet by and by'. In the sweet by and by there will be no enemies to subdue. However in this world we are surrounded by enemies of our spirit, soul and body. The time has come to understand who we are in Christ Jesus. Understand that you are the descendant of the living God, you are in him and he is in you.

Jesus said that He was in the Father and the Father was in Him and we are in Him. See Jesus on the inside of you now. You are not just natural you are a supernatural being, in the image and likeness of God Genesis 1:26. Your born again recreated spirit is immortal but you live in an earthen body. Soon the Lord will come to give you your new body which is immortal.

God is a spirit and they that worship Him must worship Him in spirit and in truth John 4:24. Only a spirit can worship God. Worship speaks of intimacy with God. To be honest, what God really wants from us is true worship. True worship brings us on the same level with God. God is seeking for true worshippers, not preachers, but worshippers.

The believer must study Genesis 1:26 -28 over and over again so that the Holy Spirit can give light on it. These words are from the mouth of the creator. Life on earth must be in light of this great mandate from the living God. Lack of knowledge in this area of knowing our true identity in Christ is the largest problem we have in the body of Christ. Most people think it is a sickness problem or a money problem but I say no. It is a lack of knowledge problem. <u>*My people are destroyed for lack of knowledge. Hosea 4:6.*</u>

The main problem is lack of knowing who God is and who we are in him also lack of knowledge of how to operate in this world with the word of God on our tongue. This is the main reason for so much failure in the body of Christ. God says we are blessed but we say we are not, and we do not line up our actions based on the word of God so, we fail time and time again to receive the things God has set for us. Keeping our eyes on the natural will help the devil whip us all the time. This is why God told us to keep his word in the midst of our heart. Proverbs 4, He said "*let them not depart from thine eyes for they are life and health to all of our flesh*". God's words are the greatest force in the world and this has always been so. This is a word planet a word responsive system however it is run by invisible spiritual forces that you can't see with your natural eyes. Study 2 Cor 4:18.

What the Lord said in Genesis 1:28 has not registered in our heart as it should. But the time has come to walk in the love of God, to walk in the wealth of God, to walk in the faith of God. Learn to operate Gen 1:28 daily.

We should always believe every word that comes from the mouth of the living God. Matthew 4:4. *Man shall not live by bread alone but by every word that comes from the mouth of God.* Remember the main man said. Take God at his word in believing what he said about you and say it all the time. We must all learn to live our lives on earth based on the word of God. <u>Descendants of God</u> must learn to walk and live like God on the earth in the here and now. Many of us believe this word about us but do not confess it out loud often. Some not at all, so we remain defeated by the enemy in our daily walk. Friend if God says you are blessed you are blessed, if he says be fruit-ful then you are because, his word is our divine ability. Whatever he says we can do then we can do it even if it means walking on water like Peter at his word "COME". Act on his word today and you will see glory power in your life. The word is the thing that will bring change to your life on earth. But you must learn to speak it daily.

<u>The power to bring the word to pass is in the word itself.</u> The power is not us so, just take God at his word no matter how things seem in this world, take Him at his word like your father Abraham. He was a very old man when God told him he would have a son and there was no hope of it taking place in the natural but God did it for him because he took God at his word. Most people are still, looking at what is going on in the seen realms but we must learn to look into the unseen world and do as the word of God says. But how do we see into the unseen? By faith with the eyes of faith you see into the unseen realms because the word tells you what is going on in the realm of the unseen. **The word is your TV into the unseen realm** of the living God. God's word tells you what is playing in the invisible world. Now understand that the invisible world is far more real that the natural world because the natural came out of the invisible world. Also, spiritual forces, spiritual laws, are superior to natural forces or natural laws. Words are spiritual force.

Satan don't want you to find out who you are in Christ, he does not want you to know you are the kin of God and Christ you are a son of God on the inside yes, you have divine status on the inside. You are far above all the power of the enemy in Christ. You are what God say you are you have what God say you have you can do what God say you can. You are seated in heavenly places in Christ Jesus Ephesians 2:6. The blessing is on you right now and it is not a feeling it is a spiritual reality in the world of the spirit where God your father is. The time has come for you to take up your divine responsibilities and do as you are commanded to do by Jesus your Lord and commanding chief.

The blessing of the Lord is for those, who obey him and take him at his word, it is for the ones who do the word daily; not just on Sundays or simply when we feel like it. But we practice the word as a lifestyle daily no matter what. Satan sends the storms so that we will not remember what God said to us in his word. He wants us to forget the word and try to sort the problems of life all by ourselves but the devil is a liar. Faith in God is taking God at his word and acting like his word is true all the time. Most of the time, all we see in the natural is completely opposite, to what the word of God say. Therefore feed your spirit with the word of God daily.

And God blessed them and said be fruit-ful and have dominion Genesis 1:28. To be blessed is to have power and authority over the enemy. It is to be equipped for what God has called us to do in this world. Jesus said look *I give you power over all the power of* the *enemy and nothing shall by any means hurt you.* Luke 10:19. With the blessing on you, you will win and excel above the storms that the enemy sends your way. Adam was master over the whole world and he ruled with the words of his mouth. <u>You can rule your world with words. Yes, with God's word in your mouth.</u> Remember how you took the word and confess your way into God's kingdom/new birth? That's the kind of power that was in the mouth of Adam before he fell into sin.

Everything had to obey the power of God's word in Adam's mouth. God created us to rule over this world and his plan is to come down and join us later. Read the last book of the bible God want to come to the earth more than how we want to go to heaven.

YOU ARE LOADED

You are the descendant of the Most High God and the reality of your status means that you are loaded with the spiritual forces of the living God within your spirit man. The same force that was in Jesus Christ is given to you in the making up of your inner man in the new birth and with the infusing of the Holy Spirit in you. This is why Jesus said I give you power over all the power of the enemy; he also said ye shall receive power after the Holy Spirit is come upon you. Let me say this again you are loaded with the spiritual forces of mercy, compassion, goodness, faith, patience, longsuffering, abundance, prosperity, success, love, hope, joy, peace, victory, kindness, gentleness and any other thing revealed in scriptures. All these forces are spiritual forces that you are loaded with and by the way you are loaded with divine healing in the atonement = at-one-ment.

You are loaded with power so confess who you are every day and the power will begin to manifest in your daily life and routine. It will take you time but don't give up keep doing the word, keep speaking the word and the spiritual forces in you will begin to explode into the natural realms. I prophesy over you in the name of the Lord Jesus Christ everything negative in your life is about to turn around. I command the wind of change to blow up on you and give you signs, miracles and wonders in Jesus Mighty Name. You are loaded with power.

<u>You are the descendant of the Most High God</u>. Do not let anything in this world rule over you but God's word which is not of this world. You were designed to live by what is not of this world so stay in the word daily. You are who God say you are not what the world system say. You are the seed of Abraham you are in the Blessing and the blessing is upon you and in you. You are **LOADED** with the **BLESSING** of the Lord. As a new creature you have it all on the inside of you right now. Psalms 3:8 Thy blessing is upon thy people Psalms 68:19. Romans 5: 17. You have the Holy Spirit in you so there is someone in you who knows all things, and he will show you things to come if you yield to him daily John 16.

Understand daily that God is a faith God and he does not function without faith. Whatsoever is not of faith is sin says the word. So make sure you are in faith if you want the Lord to respond to you. Now you do this by following his instructions in the word. His word is called the word of faith and the word of life so you can't go wrong when you stand on the word. God will never back away from his word.

Faith and life is given to us in the word of God. God does nothing without his word. The word is God and you must learn to put the word above all which it is. Even God himself submit to his word he will never break his word *Psalms 89:34 <u>My covenant will I not break nor will I alter the thing that is gone out of my lips.</u>*

<u>You notice he said the thing is gone out</u>? So the word becomes *the thing* God say's. When you speak the word it will become the thing you say as well. Your whole future is in your tongue right now. Your life will follow your mouth/your words. Jesus said <u>*you shall have what you say*</u> Mark 11:23. This is the power God has given to us as his sons. God has put miracle power in your tongue but you have to know you have it and be willing to use it. Peter said; such as I have give, I thee Acts 3 study. Friend it is already in your mouth so, say only what God say, no matter what you see in your life today.

If you want God to work for you, take him at his word and say only what he says at all times. This is where many falls down and speak against us who take God at his word. You see, <u>God will do as you say if you talk like him. This is the law of faith Num 14:28 as I live says the Lord as you have spoke in mine ears so will I do unto you.</u>

<u>When David saw Goliath he talked like God as a covenant man and God backed him up and killed his giant 1 Sam 17.</u> Your Goliath is about to die in the name of Jesus Christ. You are the descendant of the most high. You are new on the inside. You are not from down here you are born of the God of heaven. You are on assignment on the earth Jeremiah 29:11. God have a perfect plan for your life on earth.

As Jesus is at the right hand of God so are we one with him in this world 1 john 4:17. When he died you died with him, when he rose you rose with him and when he ascended you ascended with him. You are now his representative on Earth. You are his witness that he lives. Understand by faith that you are an over comer all the time because of what Jesus did for you. *Whatsoever is born of God overcomes the world 1 John 5:4.*

Faith is the victory that overcomes this world system of the devil, all the time. We are winners not losers. God only have winners.

The time has come to demonstrate the gospel of the kingdom of God to the NATIONS. This new End-time Church that the Holy Spirit is building will shake the nations of the world with the power of the Living God. **A major new anointing is coming to the body of Christ that will shake off all evil out of the Church.**

The blessing of the Lord is about to hit the body of Christ in new waves. Waves and waves of his power and glory will invade the earth realms. The body of Christ will enter into its prophetic destiny. <u>There is about to be a massive wealth transfer of wealth to the body of Jesus on the earth. This will come about in many ways new to the Church.</u>

The world will be astounded. The body of Christ will take dominion over the powers of darkness and drive it off nations and cities. The pulpit ministry is about to change for, a far more demonstrative one where men of God will demonstrate the power of Jesus Christ. Yes a new day is dawning now for the body of Christ, heaven is about to invade the earth.

There will be miracles that we have not seen before doing the impossible will be daily for the body of Christ. A special new anointing is coming on the body now for healing and wealth transfer. This is there is no turning back now. The God descendants are here. The body of Christ is about to be fully grown up, mature up in Christ. This new move of God will bring about, one of the greatest demonstration of God's power that the world has ever seen. People will develop crazy faith and operate just like Jesus Christ's in his earth walk. This is why the Lord have been teaching the body of Christ the word of faith for several years now. This word faith is about to explode and multiply and subdue the enemy and take dominion. This will be done through the church, the body of Jesus Christ in the earth today.

CHAPTER 2

YOU CARRY HIS LOVE THAT CANNOT FAIL IN YOU

God so loved the world that he gave his only begotten son that whosoever believeth in him should not perish but have everlasting life John 3:16.

The love of God is shed abroad in our hearts by the Holy Ghost which is given unto us Romans 5:6. "Behold what manner of love the Father, hath bestowed upon us that, we should be called the sons of God" 1 John 3:1.

You are a love son of the Most High God this is why you cannot fail. There is no failure in the Love of God. Jesus through his love brought his love to a dying world. You are what God say you are and, you have what God say you have. You carry his love in you right now. You are from the love country which is heaven. **_You are not of the world._** Stop talking and acting like you are from this world for by his love you are redeemed and recreated in Christ Jesus. Jesus paid the price so you could be recreated in him yes his love has connected us back to God Ephesians 1:7.

You are created in Christ Jesus the Lord, Ephesians 2:10; this is what you are full of so, you are what Jesus is. This is what you are as a son of God. Did you know that you are a partaker of the very nature of the LOVE God? 2 Peter 1:1-4 You must learn to operate in love and compassion just like Jesus did in his earth walk. Jesus is your example as to how you should walk and live in this world. Jesus was a love man in his faith walk, he was always fearless and, so must you as you take your eyes off the seen and walk in love and faith. 2 Corinthians _5:7 For_ *we walk by faith not by sight*. We don't operate by what we see in the natural but by the promises of the living God. This is what Abraham did and so must we learn to do the same. Over the years as he heard the word he stood on that word and God blessed him.

You are the true workmanship/creation/photocopy of the living God. All this powers within your inner man. This is why you are not like the world or of the world. You have the same love in you that Jesus Christ had in him in his earth walk. Jesus was the love of God in action and now it is your turn to represent him to the people you meet in your daily life journey. *As he is so are you in this world 1 John 4:17.* You are the descendant of the living God you are the very offspring of God in Christ Jesus your spirit is full of his love and fullness of his Blessing. Romans 15:29.

The love of God in action in your life is when you go share the gospel of Christ to the world Mark 15. It is a sin not to tell the world about Jesus Christ, in fact, it is wicked not to share the love of God to others. You see, what the world really needs is the love of God, in action. This love has to be poured out to them from within the body of Jesus Christ. We pour it out through the love and faith of Christ within us and we do this by faith no matter what we see about people. The Church of Christ must stop being judgmental and become problem solvers.

We will have to move from just talk now, we will have to prove to this world that Jesus is who he says he is. The word say's signs shall follow them that believe Mark 16 study. You can't stop anyone who walk in love and faith in Christ Jesus, it is impossible to stop such. Nothing is too hard for those who take God at his word and walk in the love of God. Mark 9:23 Jesus said all things are possible to him that believeth Mark 9:23.

Study and pray the word till you understand who you are in Christ and know what you carry to the world. You carry the gospel of the Kingdom to a hurting world Mark 16:15-18. You are made of what you carry within. You are internalised with the love and power of the Lord. His love nature in you is what you are really made of.

You are a partaker of his love nature. This is what you are.

You are made of love who is God so go show the world how to love. Jesus said love one another as I have loved you. Having loved his own he loved them unto the end John 13. He won't leave you part way but to the very end Matthew 28. The main thing about Jesus was his love and compassion for all that came to him. He said he that cometh unto me I will in no wise cast out. Paul said that God commended his love toward us in that while we were yet sinners Christ died for the ungodly Romans 5. Jesus died for those who put him to death on the cross. He came to set us free from the curse of the law Galatians 3:13. He said as the FATHER HATH LOVED ME EVEN SO HAVE I LOVED YOU John 15 study.

The Lord loves you no matter what kind of life you are now living. He loves you forever. You are a descendant of God, you have His love in you. This love of the Lord is within your inner man if you are born again. When you truly know who you are you cannot hate other people. Those in the Body of Christ that hates don't really know who they are in Christ. I have found that this is the largest problem in the body of Christ. *We all need to understand that we are the righteousness of God in Christ Jesus 2 Corinthians 5:21*. Learn to treat people right according to the word.

The love of God is shed abroad in our hearts by the Holy Spirit. The true love Spirit is with us all the time. The greatest force in the world is the force of Love which is God himself. It was the love of God that sent Jesus to the cross for us all. It is very important for you to know that Jesus loves you all the time and this love will never stop.

It is an everlasting love it is a forever love that is why he has drawn you to him by his spirit Jeremiah 33. *With an everlasting love have I loved thee, therefore with loving-kindness have I drawn thee.*

God has only good in his heart for you, not evil, yes his plan for you is a good plan and he wants to give you a good expected end. Jeremiah 29:11 _For I know the plans I have for you_ said the Lord, plans to do you good and not evil and to bring you to an expected end. You are the descendant of the most high and you have his love in you, yes you are his love investment to your generation he wants to love them through you. He wants to help them through you but you have to work with him you have to yield to him for this to happen.

Stop yielding to the fear of the world system and yield yourself to the Lord and his love in you. Your assignment is to carry his love to others and to the nations of the world. This is why we have to pray for others with the love of God in us. We need to understanding that God loves all people and gave Christ for all. The God we serve is the love God. The God we have is the love God. The father we have is the love father. Learn to copy him in everything you do.

You carry his love therefore you must learn to demonstrate his love to the world and to the body members of Christ. You have the right to demonstrate his love by sharing the good news with others, and laying hands on the sick so they can begin to recover. Mark 16:15-20.

You have what God says you have. You are unstoppable when you walk in love and faith who is God. God is looking for people that will love him and obey him. If you do not love him you will not obey him. We all listen to the people we love so, if we really love God we will listen to what he has to say about us. Your Blessing resides in how you listen to the Lord. This is how faith will grow in you daily. Those who listen to him will become blessed, equipped and empowered by his Spirit Gen 1:28.

Every promise in the bible is a love promise and love cannot fail, love cannot lie, and love cannot change. Love is love no matter how we feel, love is love and love is God. You CANT FAIL BECAUSE HIS LOVE IN YOU CANT, FAIL YOU. The greatest force in the universe today is love; you have this love in you in abundance. He came that you might have love and have it more abundantly. God's life is the real love life. It is perfect in all aspects of life forever. Love never fails. 1 Cor 13. Understand you carry his love in you daily and, his love can't let you down. Understand that God who lives in you, is love therefore you can't fail.

Love, who is God, is stronger than all you face today but you have to know it like David when he faced the giant. Remember that you are in a love covenant with God and covenant cannot be broken. The people who really, love God and know who, he is; cannot fail in their kingdom assignment of life.

When you know that he died for you, you can't help but love him back, but remember he loved you first. He loved you before you knew him and he loved you before he formed you in the belly Jeremiah 1. There is no need to fear or fail because the love God is with us all the time and he will never leave us or fail us. The time has come to get rid of the fear that is in the body of Christ. The time has come to walk in the fullness of the love of God letting him lead us daily so assignment will be completed. Our assignment is a love assignment to the unsaved; yes our role is to bring them back. This is why he gave us the ministry of reconciliation bringing others to him. He said tell them **"all things are now ready". Luke 14:17-23**. The blessing is ever ready to take you through the storms of life into your divine destiny and purpose.

Love has fully provided for us from the foundation of the world. Colossians 2:10 say's, we are <u>complete in him</u>. That means we are perfect in him. We are the healed in him 1 Peter 2:24. We have redemption in him, yes and we are reborn in him, so we are a new breed of love people, we are the new love generation. Being born again not of corruptible seed but of the incorruptible, by the word of God 1 Peter 1:23. Hear me well. God's love in you will see you through the storms you are in. No weapon formed against you shall prosper because love is your shield and exceeding great reward Genesis 15:1-2.

It may seem like he is sleeping but he is the Lord of your life and will not fail you, never. Your ship of life will not sink with him on board. You are about to walk on the waters of the storms of your life, you are about to go to the top in the name of Jesus. Your days of failure is over.

There is a new season of victory and Blessing coming on your life from Today. We live in a world of hate and pain but right in the midst of it there is the Love of God for those who will take it and receive eternal life the nature of God the father.

No weapon that is formed against you cannot prosper because you carry his love to the world.

You carry the greatest power in the world the Love of God in you. Understand that his omnipotent power is given to you.

It sets you apart from the system of this world that is falling apart. You are covered by his love which means you are covered by the BLESSING Galatians 3:13-14. This love of God in you will let you rise to the top all the time, regardless of what you face in your circumstances. In Christ you are a winner all the time. You are his descendant in the earth you can controls the circumstances of your daily life with his word in your mouth.

You will be tempted to operate in the flesh but don't yield to the flesh and let the devil stop your assignment. Far too many of us have abandoned the love of God for the ways of the world system. Now, learn to operate in the love of God always, like Jesus as, he never operated outside of love. Even on the cross he said "father forgive for they know not what they do".

The roman centurion said after seeing Jesus and knew how he died "this man was the son of God". The greatest thing about Jesus was his love for people and God. He was always seeking how to help others. How God anointed Jesus of Nazareth with the Holy Ghost and power who went about doing good healing all that was oppressed by the devil Acts 10:38. When you operate in the love of God the devil will not be able to stop you, on your assignment and all that you set your hands to will be blessed. Your work of faith will prosper from today in the name of Jesus **Psalms 1:3. "Thy blessing is on thy people".**

People can't stop those who carry this love of God and know what they carry. We become winners when we learn to walk in the love of the living God. The Love of God removes all condemnation that the enemy brings against us. The love of God is a doer, you can't say you love God and don't help others with this love in you. This love is 100% unselfish and seeketh not it's own but seeks to help others all the time 1 Cor 13. Jesus went looking to help the people Acts 10:38. He made himself available to take us out of our sins and sicknesses. He himself took on himself all our pains. His love would not let him pass us by. He is the Good Samaritan. He is the only good Shepherd and the great Shepherd of the sheep.

Make your life one that brings change to the world with Gods love flowing out of you daily. Take the love of God and make your mark in the world for Jesus.

Mark 16:15-20 *Go ye into all*, the world and declare the gospel to every creature. Don't Judge them, give them the gospel yes, and love them into the kingdom. Remember someone had to love you into the kingdom so now go do the same. Take the love of God and go be fruit-full and multiply and replenish people wherever you go. You have what it takes because you have his love power in you. Yes God's power in you is love power which is the greatest power in this world and the world to come.

His love in us is the power of the world to come which will function by love all the time. People on the street is waiting on you so, don't wait on a pulpit ministry go to them and bring them to Jesus. Lay your hands on them with their permission and pray for their healing. Yes on the street. Get onto the street and tell people about Jesus Christ and his love.

Share the love of the Lord with those you come in contact with. If you are his descendant you have the responsibility to share Jesus out to others. As you have received him so walk in him, which means share him out by faith. If you keep it to yourself you will get stagnant if you don't share it out you will not fulfil your purpose. You carry his love in you, you carry his power in you yes, greater is he that is in you than he that is in the world system 1 John 4:4. You have what the whole world needs so go share the love of the Lord. Ye shall receive power after the Holy Ghost is come upon you. The Holy Ghost is on you so don't be afraid or ASHAMED. <u>God said;</u> ***I will not fail thee nor forsake thee Hebrews 13:5.***

The world is waiting for those who come in the power of the love of God. The world is waiting on you. The world does not have the true love of God, it is the duty of the body of Christ to show the world the love of God. We need to learn to love people into the kingdom of God. Too many in the body of Christ is stopping others from coming to the Lord. We stand in the way of sinners with our stinking attitude that is hostile to the love and kingdom of Christ. The reason why many refuse to come to Church is because they cannot see the love of Jesus in the Church. The love of the Lord is not being displayed by those who are in the Church. Wrong, wrong, so stop it. Some of us is still bitter because of the hurts that we have been through, but now is the time to let all that go and demonstrate the love of God to a sick hurting, and dying world.

Where can the world go if not to the Church? We are the descendants of the Most High, we are born again, we are blood washed and we are what God say's we are. We have what God say's we have and we are what God say's we are. It is time for the love of God to overflow in the Church and out of the Church to those who are hurting in the world. It is time for the members of the body of Christ to stop hurting each other as we. Stop it or God will stop you.

The love of God has been trapped in the body of Christ for generations, but now the time for a new release of it to the world has come. This new release will bring about the greatest manifestation of the power of the Lord Jesus Christ that the world has ever seen. The greatest move of God through the body of Christ is upon us now a new day is dawning now. Joel 2. Don't get left behind in this great move of the Lord. *A new season of Miracles signs and wonders is here now, it is here for those who will take it by faith. Daniel 11:32.*

Now we know by the word that God is Love this is his nature love is what he is. To truly understand the nature of love who is God we need to study 1 Corinthians 13. There it is written love work no ill to its neighbour. We are living in perilous times according to 2 Peter 3 therefore the body of Christ really need to walk and live in the love of God.

This way the world will not be able to contaminate us with its evil. Love cannot be contaminated. This love is perfect all the time in all generations. God's love have no torment.

This is what we have in us but, we need to train ourselves to release it by faith. We do this as we daily seek the kingdom of God, that is inside of us. Too much focus is going to the things we see. You are a spirit so learn to live by Gods word. You must live now by what God says in his word. Every promise in the bible is a promise of love and love cannot lie. Love is full of goodness and mercy.

Love is our father, love is our mother, and love has made an eternal plan for our lives on earth and our lives in heaven. Love is a planner; the master planner. Our role in love is an eternal on not a temporary one. Love has begotten us with the word of truth we are bore again of love so this is what we are and what we carry all the time. The love of God for us knows no boundaries it is unlimited and it is eternal. This is why Jesus had to come into the world it was love that send him. He came to seek and to save that which was lost. With an everlasting love have I loved thee says the Lord. What we need today is a fresh baptism of the Love of God I think we are far too hard with each other and we need to be kingdom minded in Christ Jesus. We all need to learn to operate like Jesus. We do this by walking by faith and love. Remember, love is God and God is love. You are from the indestructible love realms Kingdom of God. This domain is within you all the time as a recreated spirit being. You are His descendant.

CHAPTER 3

LAY YOUR HANDS ON THE SICK AND THEY SHALL RECOVER

Mark 16:15-18

Go ye into the entire world, and preach the Gospel to every creature and lay hands on the sick and they shall recover. **The miracle instruction** of the Lord is very clear that he wants us to copy him by laying hands on the sick in order for him to heal them. Mark 16:15-20

How God anointed Jesus of Nazareth with the Holy Ghost and power who went about doing good healing all that was oppressed by the devil Acts 10:38. The prayer of faith shall save the sick and the Lord shall raise them up. And if they have committed sins it shall be forgiven them James 5.

Sickness is satanic oppression 100%. If it is, which it is, then it is the responsibility of the body of Christ to rebuke it back into hell where it came from. Any thing that is not coming from heaven we aught to send it back to the sender in the name of the Lord Jesus Christ. Practice doing what the word says. Be doers of the word James 1:22 in regard to getting your healing by the word of God. Just as God created the heavens and the earth with his word so your healing is realty in the realm of the spirit by the word of God.

What we need to do now is take our full stand on the healing promises of the living God. Now all of the promises of God are all omnipotent so they can't fail. You see they are really _God himself in his word_. In the *beginning was the word and the word was with God, and the word was God.* John 1:1-4. The word of God is the **force-full word** of divine healing in the atonement of Jesus Christ the son of the Living God.

To be healed we need to engraft the word into our hearts daily, this is not a fly by night thing the word must become a part of our daily life, it must be what we decide to live by all the time. As we live this way by the word, the power will be released as we speak the word, out of our hearts that is full of the word of God. <u>*Let them not depart from thine eyes but keep them in the midst of thine heart. Proverbs 4. They are health to them that find them*</u>.

God is not the one that put sickness on people but the devil Acts 10:38 how God anointed Jesus of Nazareth with the Holy Ghost and with power who went about doing good healing all that were oppressed of the devil for God was with him.

But the work of the body of Christ is to take it off people with the power in the mighty name of Jesus. In my name lay hands on the sick is the command of the Lord. The church must understand that it is always the will of God to heal all because this is why he has put his supernatural power in your hands yes fire is in your hands, <u>so believe it is and, it will work to heal the sick.</u>

Jesus paid the price for our healing with his blood and his stripes 2000 years ago. If we are, still doubting, it will not work because, it is your faith you have to use to receive the healing from the word of God which is the word of faith. There are so many lies the devil has fed into us that we are still thinking it is not the will of God for us to be well all the time and that God uses sickness to help us. This is a lie from hell to stop the body of Christ. It is a lie against the truth of the word of the living God. James 3:14.

The body of Christ must now learn to stop lying against the truth of the word of God revealed so clear in scripture we must embrace the will of

God for our healthy fully. This plan of God for our health has always been in his word *Jeremiah 29:11. For I know the plans I have for you saith the Lord*. The time has come to stop focusing on the lies of the devil and focus on the word of the living God. He sent his word and healed them and delivered them from their destructions Psalms 107:20 Gods word is not the product of time nor is it from this world but God's word is God himself concerning our total life on earth.

Healing is not an after thought with God it was his will from the very start that we should live our lives on the earth in perfect health .When Adam sold out God spoke his healing word unto us through the prophetic word of faith. God has also put healing on our tongue. Your health is actually on your tongue right now so it is up to you what you say. Speak sickness away.

Matthew 10:1:1 And when he had called his disciples he gave them power against unclean spirits to cast them out and to heal all sicknesses and all manner of disease.

This scripture gives a lot of detail into the mind of the Lord Jesus regarding sickness and dealing with devils. If you take a close look in the word of God you will notice that sickness and disease is always closely linked to the activities of devils. Jesus said in my name cast out devils. This is what we must do in order to become successful in the things of the kingdom of God. Sickness is a spirit that must come under the hammer of the word of God in our mouth. Jesus said **"I will be thou clean"** and healing burst forth instantly. The same will take place in your life shortly in the name of Jesus. Just focus on getting the healing word into your heart and keep it there, then as you speak you will see the glory of the Lord in your life.

And when he had called to him his disciples he gave them power against unclean spirits to cast them out and to heal all manner of sickness and all manner of disease Heal the sick that are there in Luke 10:9.

Jesus not only healed the sick but showed his disciples how to heal them with his word as well. How did he do it? He did by the power of the Holy Spirit with the words of his mouth. John 6:63. The words that I speak they are Spirit and they are life. The church should never be afraid to do as the Lord say because if he said it, he will do it no matter what things look like in the natural.

Jesus. If we obey him he will show us his healing power. Remember God cannot work in your life without your permission this is the way he has set up his word of faith system. All you need to do is what he told you in his word. For those of you who are sick in your bodies please get your eyes of the flesh and unto the word of the living God which you will find in the Bible. Get by your self and study the healing promises. After you know the will of God which is to heal you don't stop speaking it to the problem day and night. One day you will rise up from sleep and the sickness will be gone.

Plus your faith life will grow as a result of you daily acting on the word and speaking the word out daily to your problems. Forget the opinion of people around you and stay with the word all the time and you will get your, healing. Agree with God believe his word and confess it out of your mouth without shame and you will see God do as you say all the time. Yes the sick will be healed before your eyes. Agree -believe –confess.

I have seen this many times as I apply the word to the problems I face in my life and ministry. Do not worry about how it works, just trust the Lord to do as he said he will do if we do as he said. Understand that it is always the will of God to heal always every time anywhere you go. Don't let people that don't know the word put you off by saying it will not work because, you already know that God cannot lie to his people.

The scriptures cannot be broken. It is your job to demonstrate the <u>power you have in you</u> daily to the world. The supernatural life of God is dwelling inside of you. The word say Jesus healed them all so stop making excuses and lay hands on the sick so they can recover. God will keep his part of the covenant if you keep your part. Every where Jesus went he was doing good not one was turned away Acts 10:38. We must do the same as he did in his earth walk because this is what we are called to do with His mighty Spirit in us. We are far too passive in the body of Christ it is time to take action against the enemy and drive him out of what God has given us in Christ. A healthy body is our divine right in the covenant. <u>Prosperity is our legal right</u>. Put pressure on the word and take your portion. You do this by speaking the word at least three times a day very often. This must be done as a life style to get rapid results; this is the secret.

People are dying and they need you now. You were born for this. You can make the difference, things don't, have to stay the same. This is why God sent you to the earth to help others with his power in you. Jesus said "Lay hands on the sick". Mark 16:15-18. Sickness should not be in our lives, home or Church. Healing is a part of the Blessing of Abraham. Wholeness is a part of the blessing. Jesus healed the people. Sickness is a spirit out of the pit of hell that needs to be driven back with the power of the Lord in our mouth. God has put his word in your mouth to break out of sickness but you must be consistent with it. Too many when prayed for is not healed because of the lack of standing on the word of God.

This is not right for God and His word are one and God cannot lie to His people. If we really stand on the word we will see the power of God flowing out of us. The main reason things don't work is because we don't really believe it will work when we pray. But it is impossible for the word not to work when we do things after God's order. God's word never changes his laws can't change. As descendant of God you have all power over sickness and diseases.

You can't change natural laws so you can't change the law of the word of God. It is us that must come in line with the word of God. It is time for the Church to act like Jesus in the Earth. Lay hand s on the sick and they shall recover Stop going by how things look, or how you feel.

Believe God and act on his word and you will see the glory of the Lord. The Lord says the Just shall live by his faith. When we learn to walk by faith as descendants of God we cannot go under. Remember what God told Paul "it shall be as it was told you Acts 27:25".

No matter how it looks right now what God told you is still the truth and the truth has creative power that will work for you. *<u>Jesus said you shall know the truth and the truth shall set you free</u>. John 8:32. Sickness is a truth but the word of God is the truth. The real truth is what God says in his word.*

Jesus always healed the sick when they came to him, not one person was sent away the bible said he healed them all. Acts 10:38 say's How God anointed Jesus of Nazareth with the holy Ghost and with power who went about doing good healing all that was oppressed by the devil, for God was with him. Therefore we see that sickness is a curse not a blessing and that is why Jesus took it off those who came to him for healing. Now who did Jesus obey always?

Jesus said, 'I do always those things that please the father'. Jesus said in the garden not my will but thine be done, so you see him doing only what the father wanted. With that in mind remember it is his will for you to take the healing that he has already given you in his word by faith. *He sent his word and healed then and delivered them from their destructions. Psalms 107:20.* <u>Lay hands on the sick and they will be healed.</u> These are the days that we will see great signs from heaven as we preach the unlimited Word of the living God.

Mighty miracles will take place as the body of Christ press into who we are in Christ. This revelation will break more and more in the body globally a new remnant is rising up and taking our place in Christ. There will be mass healing in the local Church. There is a new anointing coming to, the local Church for the healing of the sick. Get ready for it. Sick people should never be turned away by the Church they should get their healing. The Church has been hiding from its duty for far too long the time has come to be bold and daring with Gods word in our mouths.

Now the Lord is calling us to learn to walk by faith on a daily basis. You carry His power to heal the sick, no sickness should be in our body so rebuke it now release the power of God against it now for by His stripes we are healed. It is already done in the realms of the spirit so <u>take it by faith in God.</u>

It is the word that does the healing; there is no healing outside of the word of God. God heals when men take him at his word and act like it is true. The word is spirit and they are life. John 6:63. When you release the word you are releasing new life. Now God word in your mouth is miracle power just as when Jesus spoke it 2000 years ago. God put you as a new creature not under any oppression of Satan so take dominion and strike at the enemy with what God has given you to use. Moses had to use the rod in order to get results and now you will have to learn to use the word of God on your tongue to get the sick healed by the power of the living God.

God's word cannot change because the nature of the word is eternal just like God yes the word is God. In the beginning was the word and the word was with God and the word was God John 1:1.There is nothing in this world that can defeat the word of God in your mouth. So speak the word to the things you face daily and they will have to come in line with what you say.

Many in the body of Christ were taught that the days of healing are over when the first leaders in the Church died but this is not so because Jesus is the same <u>yesterday today and forever Heb 13:8</u>. His will and purpose never changes and the word of God who is God never changes. The only safe place to find out what the will of God is the written word of God and Jesus said to the leper in ***Matthew 8:1-3.*** <u>***I will be thou clean and he put his hands on him and healed him.***</u>

You notice how Jesus put forth his hand and touch the man in order to release the healing? You can do the same for you are his representative on the earth. <u>Be clean is God's will for all men in all time</u>. There is no sickness in heaven there is no pain in heaven because God is in total control but on earth dominion was given to man. What a mess we have made of this world.

Gen 1:28 God gave the control over all the earth to man. Genesis 1:26. "He said let them have dominion" and *Jesus said, "behold I give you power over all the power of the enemy. Luke 10:19"*. We have to be real stupid to miss that but that is what we have done over many years THE ENEMY has blinded the body of Christ to our true authority and power in Christ over sickness and disease. Find out who you are in Christ and think on it daily. The body of Christ must take the healing power of the Lord to the nations of the world. Proving that Jesus Christ is Lord.

The healing ministry of the Church is the greatest way to win new people into the body of Christ. The kingdom will expand greatly when we walk as Jesus walked in his earth walk. 1 John 2:6. We are to, walk Just like Jesus, we are to follow in the footsteps of faith like the master. We are to **walk in the same steps of faith** like Abraham Romans 4:12.

We are sent to the nations according to mark 16:15-20 Jesus said "***go ye into all the world and preach the gospel***" (gospel mean good news) to every creature. So we see that, the Lord wants us to tell all of his love for them, and this must be done in a demonstrative way with signs and wonders. Our role is to proclaim the word and the Lord will confirm it with signs following. We are for miracles signs and wonders this is what we are for in this world just like Jesus was when he walked the earth. Acts.2:22.The Church is approved of God to carry on what the second Adam started. ***Jesus said as the father hath sent me even so send I you. John 20:21.***

He said we are not of the world but we are sent to the world to re-present him to a dying world blinded by Satan. We are to turn them from darkness to light by demonstrating the word of God to the people of the world. Jesus said these signs shall follow them that believe. In my name shall they cast out devils they shall lay hands on the sick and they shall recover. Not die but recover. This is what will happen when we believe the word of the Lord and act on it always as a lifestyle.

It is our responsibility as a kingdom representative/ citizens to demonstrate to the world the <u>power of the Holy Spirit we have in us</u> to the hurting the world. People are suffering all over the world but we can't help with the power of the Lord yes we can help with the power of the fullness of the blessing of Jesus Christ manifesting through us daily. We can do all things through Christ Jesus who strengthens us to fulfil purpose and destiny.

Peter said, such as I have give I the, in the name of Jesus Christ of Nazareth rise up and walk. Acts 3. What Peter had in him is in you also. What Peter did we can do because we have the same hope of glory in us the same Holy Spirit is in us. We are the **supernatural race** of the living God in the earth today. Jesus has given back to us all what Adam lost in the garden. The supernatural life of God is dwelling inside of you. The word says Jesus healed them all so, stop making excuses and lay hands on the sick so they can recover and the Lord will get the glory.

Every where Jesus went he was doing good. When we make ourselves available so the Lord, Can use us, we are doing a good work. Healing is good, sickness is evil and satanic and it's the curse in action illegally. Jesus stopped the sickness when all came to him and we must do the same with His mighty Spirit in us. We are far too passive in the body of Christ it is time to take action against the enemy and drive him out with what God has given us to use. We have been given the name of Jesus by Jesus himself. A healthy body is our divine right in the covenant. <u>Prosperity is our legal right in the covenant. Poverty is anti-covenant so curse it so, it will die.</u>

Nations are dying and they need us now. As a new creature in Christ Jesus you were born for this you are equipped by the Holy Spirit for this. You can make the difference in this world with God's word in your mouth. Things don't, have to stay the same so take God's power and change things. This is why God sent you to the earth to help others with his power in you. Ephesians 2:10 God planned your life on earth ahead of time so enjoy the ride because you are a winner all the time in Christ Jesus.

Jesus said "lay hands on the sick and they shall recover." Mark 16:15-18.

Sickness should not be in our lives because we are God's covenant people God's home, God's Church. Healing is a part of the blessing of Abraham and the blessing has come on us through Jesus Christ. Wholeness is a part of the blessing of Abraham. Jesus healed the people. Sickness is a spirit out of the pit of hell that needs to be driven back with the power of the Lord in our mouth.

Too many when prayed for is not healed because they don't believe. This is not right for God and His word are one and God cannot lie to His people. If we really stand on the word we will see the power of God flowing out of us. The main reason things don't work is because we don't really believe it will work when we pray. But it is impossible for the word not to work when we do things after God's order.

God's will and nature never changes so his laws can't change. It is us that must come in line with the word of God. It is time for the Church to act like Jesus in the Earth. Lay hand s on the sick and they shall recover, Stop going by how things look, or how you feel. Believe God and act on his word and you will see the glory of the Lord. Mark 9:23All things are possible to him that believeth. The Lord says *the Just shall live by his faith.* Hebrews 10:38 When we learn to walk by faith as descendants of God we cannot go under.

Remember what God told Paul "*it shall be as it was told you Acts 27:25*". Lay hands the sick and they shall recover Mark16:15-20on. No matter how it looks right now what God told you is still the truth and the truth has creative power that will work for you. Jesus said you shall know the truth and the truth shall set you free.

Now you must spend time with the Lord so you can develop in these things because it is not by observation but by faith in God that you walk with God. The more you get the healing word into your mouth and heart the more you will see the power of the Lord flowing out of you and meeting the needs of people around you daily.

No matter what happens you are to remember that you are the descendant of the Most High God and you have his life and power in you to get the job done.

The only reason why you are laying your hands is because this is what the Lord wants you to do so don't be afraid. The Holy Spirit lives in you so you have all the power.

Stop talking like the devil and start talking like Jesus Christ

You are not as weak as the devil wants you to think and say. Satan wants you to focus on the problems you have but God wants you to focus on his word to you. God says we are healed so don't let that word depart from your eyes no matter what you experience in your body or what you see people have in their body. We walk by faith not by sight 2 Corinthians 5:7 If we walk by sight by what we see in this world we will never be able to take, what is our property. Faith is a way of life a way of living, never forget this fact. **Your healing is already yours.**

<u>Lay hands on the sick and they shall recover.</u> Recovery is sure if we do as God say. He said "<u>I am the Lord that healeth thee</u>". Exodus 15:26. Stand on this word and expect God to show up for you always. Go lay hands on the sick and pray by faith. These are the days that we will see great signs from heaven as we preach the word of the Lord. Mighty miracles will take place as the body of Christ press into who we are in Christ. This revelation will break more and more in the body of Christ

globally. There will be mass healing in the local Church. There is a new anointing coming to the local Church for the healing of the sick. Get ready for it. Sick people should never be turned away by the Church they should get their healing. Get ready for wealth transfer as well.

Wealth is about to be released to the body of Christ yes wealth without limit. The treasures of darkness are about to be handed over to the body of Christ big time. There will be new inventions and ideas that will blow the minds of many. The Church has been hiding from its duty for, far too long. Knowledge will increase to astounding levels the nearer the coming of the Lord.

As wickedness increases, the glory of the Lord will be released within the body of Christ, preparing his Church for his return. He is not coming for a weak Church but for a strong mature Church. Our best days are ahead of us now this is it, the Lord is coming soon. Now the Lord is calling us to learn to walk by faith on a daily basis. You carry His power in you to heal the sick, no sickness should be in your body so rebuke it yes veto it with the blood of Jesus.

Release the power of God against it now for by His stripes we are healed. Isaiah 53:5. You carry His joy in you daily so why are you, so sad, start to praise Him now and glory fire will fall on you right now. Praise him daily for his mercy and you will stir his Joy in you. Remember the Joy of the Lord is your strength. There are too many miserable people in Church. You are putting people off for too long now.

You carry His prosperity in you daily yes, you do for, the blessing of the Lord maketh rich and it addeth no sorrow. God's greatest wish is that you will prosper and be in health as your soul prospers. If your soul doesn't prosper, you will not be able to prosper in what you do in life. <u>Your soul has to prosper and you do that by meditation on the word and prayer daily.</u>

<u>Healing is a part and parcel of the Gospel of Jesus Christ Matthew 8:16-17. The enemy is attacking the people of God with much sickness and the time has come to resist the devil with God's word in our mouth.</u> Sickness is anti covenant, it is not of God, it is not a part of the blessing, it is a curse of the law. But Christ hath redeemed us from the curse of the law.

Therefore, sickness has no right to be in our bodies which now belong to the Lord. Our bodies are the sole property of the Lord Jesus Christ so sickness should not lord it over us. The time has come to veto sickness out of the body of Jesus Christ. In Mark 6 Jesus sent his disciples out to preach and to heal the people.

They went and they cast out devils and healed the sick. What did they do? They laid their hands on the sick and anointed them with oil and prayed over them. Mark 6:13. So even when the Lord was walking on earth we were praying over the sick and anointing with oil at his instruction and God healed the people. The word say's the prayer of faith shall save the sick, James 5 and friend God has not changed his mind about our healing. That which is gone out of the lips of the Lord will not be altered in any way. <u>*Psalms 89:34 My covenant will I not break*</u>.

No one can change God's word not even God himself can't do that. It is written I am the Lord I change not. We lay hands on the sick on the basis of God's eternal word that is surer than any thing we see in the natural. God's word is not subject to change or time the word is above all. The word is alive pulsating with life/power Heb 4:12.

Psalms 138:2 Thou hast magnified thy word **<u>*above all thy name*</u>. We must do the same on earth.**

There is no one above, the word of God even God submits to his own word.

God's word is supernatural eternal law over sickness and disease there is no sickness that can withstand the word of faith in our mouth. Therefore speak it.

The Lord clearly instructed his Church to pray for the sick and to lay hands on the sick and they shall recover. Problem is the Church has been hiding from the way of faith for years. We have been hiding within the world system of fear and doubt yet looking for God to work for us. No God will only respond to your faith.

I believe the time has come for a radical change as to how we think in the body of Jesus Christ. We should no longer let what belongs to us in Christ go from us. We must stop letting the devil steal from us the things that God has given to us in his word. Jesus spent a lot of his ministry healing the sick to show us for all time that it is God's will for the sick to receive their. "He said <u>"I will be thou clean" Matthew 8:1-2</u>.

There is supernatural power in your hands to heal the sick so don't be afraid just do as the Lord say's. Start looking for people not in church to pray for. Find them on the streets God will heal as you pray. This is one way you can win many into the kingdom. *Ye shall lay hands on the sick and they shall recover. Mark 16:15-20.*

All sick people have the right to be healed because of what Jesus did for us all. The body of Christ is already healed but we have to take it from the spirit realms with our faith in God's eternal promises. Yes the healing is there to be taken by our faith in the word who is Jesus. Believe in your heart that it is already done and you will see the power working for you A new wave of the healing glory of the Lord is about to hit the body of Jesus Christ. It will flow like a mighty river and heal the sick.

Healing comes to us as we act on the word of God as a lifestyle yes, God's word in our mouth becomes <u>what we say healing health prosperity etc. Please don't forget this; God's word in your own mouth will turn into healing for your body. His word will save you from your sicknesses and destructions Psalms 107:20 *He sent his word and healed them and delivered them from their destructions.*</u>

Did you know that the word says God's word is medicine to all your flesh? Proverbs 4:20-23.The word health means medicine in Hebrews. So as we meditate the word it becomes our health and wealth and so forth. The greatest force in the world has always been the miracle working word of God in the mouth of man. Supernatural power is given to us in our mouth. Numbers 14:28 They were not even born again, yet there was power in their mouths.

Lay hands on the sick and they shall recover. This is the duty of the Church it is a divine assignment of the body of Christ and it will draw others to Jesus when the sick are healed by his power.

We can't heal anyone but we have the healer in us and, he will heal the sick in line with his word in our mouth. Always say what God says about your health stop talking about how you feel all the time and say what the word says about your situation. God's power is released only after we obey him by faith that means, before we see any change in the natural, we simply, do as God says in his word. In the kingdom of God there is no sickness or pain so we have the right to veto it when the enemy brings it against our bodies.

Understand that the work that Jesus started, we must continue until he comes back, this is what we are called to do as the global Church of Jesus Christ. Mark 16:15-20. Most people in the Church are sick and this is not right because, we have the healer living in us. The time has come to know who we really are, and what we have in us. We have the hope of glory living forever in us and he lives in us to put us over not under because we are the head AND NOT THE TAIL Colossians 1:27 Deuteronomy 28:1-14 study. We are what God say's we are, not what the devil say's, not what sickness says. We are healed by his stripes. **We are his <u>descendant</u>s on the earth today.**

We are about to see some of the greatest signs that man have ever seen from heaven. The laying on of hands so the sick can be healed is a major ministry the Lord has given to the body of Christ. All believers can do this not just those at the front of ministry. We all have the right to cast out sickness spirits and to get the sick healed in the name of Jesus. Matthew 8:16. Mark 16:15-20. As we use the method that the Lord gave to us we will see him work wonders in these final days of time. He will confirm his word with signs miracles and wonders.

The body of Christ have been operating far too low, in the power the Lord has given to us to help those who are sick. We have not been acting on his word as we should to get the sick healed. But the word still says; *such as I have give I thee,* Acts 3. Lay hands on the sick and they shall recover mark 16, so, look for opportunities to pray for the sick so the Lord can get glory by healing them.

When you pray for the sick remember that, in the realms of the invisible they are already healed so use the word to build their faith then, lay your hands on them and give the faith command in Jesus mighty name. When Jesus went to the cross he took all our sins and sickness to the cross, so what he took we don't have to bear any longer because he paid the price with his blood for our victory over sin and sicknesses. Matthew 8:17.

<u>Put pressure on the word for healing wherever you go</u> and the Lord will back his word that you speak. Yes when you keep speaking the word which is the language of God he will show you his power. It will not flow if you are not sure. It will stay if you do not believe, but if you believe and keep saying it and act on the word you will see great release of the healing power of the Lord in your life to help many others.

You are dealing with invisible powers when you are praying over the sick so stand fast on the word of God and do not back off. Keep doing what the word says in regard to healing as a lifestyle. Lay hands on the sick and they shall recover.

I dare you to act daily on the word of God and you will see the glory of the Lord in your life. Healing will break out in your life and ministry as you do and, the Lord will get the glory. Healing the sick is a divine right that is given to us as we act on the word of faith that we hear daily. Faith to be healed comes as we keep listing to what God has to say about our health in his word. He said; *I WILL BRING IT HEALTH AND CURE.* Don't let Satan con you out of what is your birthright blessing. Healing is so much yours that you can give it away to others, if they will accept in by Faith in the name of the Lord Jesus. Always remember you are in the Kingdom of Christ in your spirit man so that is where you are. Therefore, sickness has no power over you. Your tongue is over all sickness and they must obey your voice of faith. 1 Peter 2:24 "By His stripes ye were healed". If we were healed then, we are healed right now in the name of the Lord Jesus Christ.

When you are praying for the sick, get them to act on the word that, you must show them. It is as they act on the word the power will start to flow, and they will be healed by the power of the Holy Spirit in the name of Jesus. Make sure you give all the Glory to Jesus all the time and he will show you more of his great power. This power is already in you, you don't have to pray for it, all you need to do is know that you have it on your tongue all the time and use it in Jesus name. It will flow out of your mouth as you speak. It is invisible but it is real and it is a part of your inner man where God lives in your all the time. You are the **descendant of the living God**. 1 John 4:4. Friend go lay hands on the sick and rebuke that sickness out of them in Jesus name.

CHAPTER 4

YOU CARRY HIS BLESSING UPON YOU RIGHT NOW

Psalms 3:8, "Thy blessing (is) ***upon thy people***".

Galatians3:13-14 "Christ hath redeemed us from the curse of the law, being made a curse for us because it is written cursed is everyone that hang on a tree, that the blessing of Abraham might come on the gentiles/nations through Jesus Christ that we might receive the promise of the spirit through faith.

Gen 12:1-3 "I will bless/empower thee and thou shall be a blessing and in thy seed all nations of the earth shall be bless" (study).You are blessed to be a blessing to other people.

You are blessed just like faithful Abraham. You are Abraham's seed so it means you are in covenant with the living God. You are redeemed from the curse to the blessing. Sickness poverty lack and famine is not your portion because you are redeemed from them. The blessings make you rich now. The blessing is your shepherd you shall not want. The blessing is your healer so you don't have to stay sick. The blessing is your future so you don't have to worry. The blessing is stronger than "He that is in the world". You need to understand that the blessing is God Himself empowering you daily. You are rich. You are strong. You shall have what you say. Mark 11:23.

You need to understand that the blessing is the ability of God on your life. It lifts you out of the normal and brings you into the supernatural of God. The same Peter that swore and turned his back on Jesus took the blessing and turned the world upside down. There was a man lamed from birth but with the blessing the lame started to walk just like how Jesus did it. You see Jesus is really the Blessing. Peter walked on water because the blessing told him to "come". Peter preached 3000 into the Kingdom with one sermon Acts 2.

The blessing led him to the house of Cornelius and saved Cornelius his home and his friends. You carry the same blessing. The blessing is the life force of God in man. The blessing has no limit. He will give you miracles if you stay in the blessing. You have what the world needs badly. They need the blessing real bad.

The lame can walk, the blind can see if you work with the blessing. You have to know who you are. Satan is afraid of the blessing. It was the blessing that killed Goliath, it was not David. But David had to speak in line with what God had said about himself. You have to do the same. Say what God told you no matter what you see. The blessing wants to show up in your life and family. The blessing is personal and generational.

You carry the blessing that was on Adam before he fell. Then Noah and Abraham, Isaac, Jacob and Joseph, all Israel. And all because of Jesus, the same blessing is on you. You are the seed of Abraham you are an heir of the blessing. Galatians 3:29 "And if ye be Christ's, then are ye Abraham's seed, and heirs according to the promise". The secret of success on earth is to receive the highest authority that heaven can give which is the blessing. There is <u>nothing in this life superior to the blessing</u>. With the blessing we have power with God and man and we have power over the devil with the blessing on us. With the blessing we are absolutely unstoppable just like David against Goliath and Gideon against the Midianites.

The blessing <u>turns us into supernatural people</u>. Man was never meant to live on the earth without the blessing because purpose is impossible to be fulfilled with the blessing. You cannot arrive at your divine destiny without the blessing empowering your life. It is the blessing that was on Jesus Christ the son of God that causes Him to be so effective in His earth walk. Jesus relied totally on the power of the blessing in His earth walk, now we as believers must learn to recognise the blessing in the word of God that is on us, that is in us and walk in it daily.

With the blessing on our lives we come God's supernatural people, we can plunder hell and populate heaven with the gospel of Jesus Christ, remember that the gospel of Christ in your mouth is the power of God unto salvation/healing/deliverance/success/miracle living. The gospel of Christ brings man back into the realms of God and the gospel is the blessing of God on man.

The purpose of God is to blessing man to empower man not to bring man down but the purpose of the devil is to kill, steal and destroy. Understand that you have power absolute power over satanic forces with the blessing on you. You can ambush satanic forces with your strategic prayers and your strategic confession of the word of God night and day regarding your circumstance or the things you desire. The enemy have no control over those that carry the blessing unless we give him place through ignorance and disobedience. That's why the word said "give no place to the devil and resist the devil and he will flee from you" James 4:7.

The words of the blessing that we speak daily will absolutely set us free and manifest our turn around and the words of the enemy will bind us and keep us in satanic bondage. This is why we must study the word until we are approving of God so we can divide the word of God properly and rightly. What is needed in the body of Christ is for the believer to handle the indestructible word of the blessing by the faith of God. You see God respects no man but He respect faith, that's why he told the sinner Centurion as thou as believed so be it done unto thee Matt 8:13, he was not a part of the body of Christ at that time, but his spirit tapped into the spirit of God and the ability of the spoken word and Jesus Christ gave him and his servant an astounding miracle. With the blessing on your life having your cooperation nothing can stop you, no Jordon, no Red Sea, no Giant, no sickness, no financial pressure, no relationship pressure, no storms of life is able to stop those who carry the blessing and recognise what we have and who we are, and whose we are.

Thy blessing is upon thy people Psalms 3:8. Something invisible is on you.

With the Blessing you carry all of Him daily. 1 John 4:17
With the blessing you carry His divine life in you St John 10:10.
With the blessing you carry His good news daily Mark 10:15-18.
With the blessing you carry His wisdom in you daily 1 Corinthians 1:30.
With the blessing you carry His power in you daily Luke 10:19.
With the blessing you carry His wealth in you daily Proverbs 10:22.
With the blessing you carry His name with you daily Mark 16:15-18.

The time has come for us to awake out of our sleep and shine with the gospel of Christ in us. We want to help others with this power and blessing that the Lord has given to us. Potipher saw that the Lord was with Joseph. Saul saw that the Lord was with David, God's dominion mandate for man has never change. Jesus reiterated this by saying "I give you power over all the power of the enemy and nothing shall by any means hurt you." Luke 10:19.

That sounds like Genesis 1:28 to me. Be fruit-ful multiply replenish the earth subdue control and have dominion so you can clearly see that man ought to reign over the earth in the name of the Lord. I see you reigning now in the name of Jesus.

Man in Christ is a son of God a new creation in Christ Jesus. In Christ you have been given divine status Col .3:1. If any man be in Christ he is a new creature old things are passed away and behold all things are become new. That which is born of the spirit is spirit. Understanding your place of power and authority in Christ is vital to operating in your privileges in him. This is the way your purpose and destiny will be fulfilled.

In your spirit man you are like Adam before he sinned. You are the body of Christ in the earth. You are an eternal spirit born of the Most High God. You are his child you are the offspring of God almighty. This is what you are weather you feel like it or not and no man can change this. There is no condemnation on you because you are born of the Lord God in Christ Jesus. Romans 8:1.

You are spirit of His spirit; you are divine because He is divine. You are righteous because He is righteous; you are the branch of the divine vine. You are the fruit burning part of God. His Zoë life, His nature, His being, His substance of life is within you. Because you are His, you carry the glory on the inside of you. You carry His anointing in you and on you. You carry on the inside the potential of Jesus Christ because you have the spirit, you have His power (Dunamis) internalised into, when you got born again John 1:12 yet to all who receive Him to those who believe in his name He gave the right to become children of God. You are the breed that has power over all the power of the enemy Luke 10:19, Matt 10:1, Acts 1:8.

You cannot be defeated because you have already won in Christ. All the enemy is trying to hold back from you is already yours. Jesus paid for your new birth and all the honours and rights of the blood covenant that comes with it. His blood is now yours all the power in His blood now belongs to you. His blood speaks better things for you. You are a wonder to the world and to the Angels. You are a sign to the world. Your time has come so shine on in the name of Jesus. All things are now possible because you know who you are in Him. The enemy is afraid of you and what you have on the inside. You can now stop him dead in his tracks. You now have power and authority over him and all his demons.

You are unstoppable so act like it every day

In all these things we are more than conquerors Rom 8:32. You are unstoppable, Mark 16:17 because you belong to the God kind of beings, the God kind of race, Acts 17 as He is so are we in this world 1 John 4:17. Look at the life of Peter who was so afraid to own Christ before he was filled with the Holy Spirit. After he was filled and really found out who he was the man was a power house with no devils able to stop him. He was no longer afraid of death it self. In Acts 12 when Herod was planning to kill him and therefore put him in prison till the morning instead of Peter staying up and praying for God to save him from death the same peter was now fast asleep in the prison.

It was the church who had to do the praying to get him out. A new boldness came on Peter after he began to understand the things that Jesus was showing him for over three years. When we really find out who we are in Christ the devil will have a lot of retreating to do from the body of Christ. I believe with all my heart that we are about to step into that arena now because the shaking has started in the world and the body of Christ. Every thing that can be shaken is now being shaken by the power of the Lord.

I see you crushing the enemy under you feet in Jesus name I see your days of stagnation coming to an end, in Jesus mighty name. I bind the strongman operating. Nothing will be able to stop the informed body of Jesus Christ nothing. The wisdom of God is about to rise up in the body of Christ to levels that will astound the whole world. The people of the world will wonder where we come from because all we say will come to pass. Where new technology fail the body of Christ will not fail because of the fresh anointing coming on the body of Christ. We shall be anointed with fresh oil that will let the impossible become possible. I heard **Pastor Penny Francis** said "when God made us in heaven he did not put any impossibility on us it was the devil who put labels on us down here". As far as God is concerned all things are possible to him that believeth.

No weapon form against you shall prosper in the name of our Lord Jesus. I see you operating in the fullness of the blessing of the gospel of

Jesus Christ. Hear me my friends most of us attend Church, we pray sing, read the bible but we have not yet accept who we are in Christ. We embrace the tradition of man rather than embracing the word of truth. However for us to see God at work in us and through us, we must learn to take God at His word. You see faith is only activated when we act upon the word regardless of our circumstances 1 John 3:3.

The Law of Faith Confession is, you shall have what you say Mark 11:23.

Learn the language of God and use it daily. If we are the sons of God we must have His awesome potential on the inside. The time has come to go back to the principles of Genesis 1 where God showed us how to get things done by speaking them out of our hearts what we put in it. This is the LAW. You put things in your heart by meditating and speaking them. <u>Proverbs 23:7, as you thinketh in your heart so are you.</u>

Solomon said "keep you heart with all diligence, for out of it springs the issue of life. You are designed by God to get only what you speak out of your mouth. You intimidate the devil with the words of your mouth. Nobody can stop you except you.

Three million Jews could not stop two men in the wilderness because they said what God said about themselves, they knew that God could not fail them. They knew that somehow God would show up and bring his promise of the promise land to pass.

You need to reach the place where you know that God is on your side and no matter what; He will take you over Joshua 1 "<u>Be strong and of good courage says the Lord</u>, I will take you over". Fear thou not.

You are God's investment to your generation, you are special because He is special, and He shares His life with you. He is King, so you are a royal divine being on the Earth capable of operating like Jesus in the world. Many of us have never meditated on these things so as to get them into our spirit and live by them.

But I see you walking in them now by faith in the name of Jesus Christ. Learn to operate in the power like Jesus did, "greater is He that is in you than he that is in the world".

Rise up, take authority and rule over the enemy

The power is within you; you are a born again spirit man so you can make it despite the lies of the enemy. You have already won because Jesus is the victory. You will make it. As a son, the joy of the Lord is your strength. I cannot understand how some Christians have no joy. Something is wrong, that's all I will say about that. You have the greatest person in the universe living in you now. Yes, the very same Holy Spirit that was in Jesus Christ, the son of the living God. This is the moment of your manifestation step into your destiny it is calling you.

Man in Christ can operate just as how God did in Genesis 1. Why? It is because you are after God's kind. I see you rising up and taking charge of your divine status in Christ Jesus. I see you stepping into dumbfounding breakthroughs in all areas of your life; things are about to change tremendously in your life. Your stagnation is over in the name of Jesus. Take your place in the Kingdom and do great exploits for the Glory of God. To you dear ones as it is written in Isaiah 54:17 "No weapon formed against you shall not prosper. Did you hear that? All the weapons in this world can't defeat you, because you have the Kingdom of God in you. You are the one in charge, not the devil Luke 10:19 "I give you power over all the power of the enemy and nothing shall by any means hurt you".

Did you know that the Kingdom rules over all? Psalms 103:19. We take the word of God and rule over the seen and unseen things of this world. Sons of God carry the keys of the Kingdom; the keys are already in your hands. Rise up by the faith of God and use the Kingdom principle keys that you have been given. Rise like Joshua and smite your enemy in the spirit world with the weapons of spiritual warfare. Rise up and bind the strongman that has been hindering your progress. Bind him now in the name of Jesus Matt 18. Our victory over the enemy is so complete that God said he prepares a table before us in the present of our enemies. Think about this.

Ephesians 1:7 in whom we have redemption through His blood even the forgiveness of sins. Man in Christ is man restored back to dominion and put back into the garden of the Kingdom. Just as if sin had never been we are back again, redeemed out of the hand of a cruel enemy that has no mercy. By the grace of God we are back in the family of The Most High God. We have the garden back. We are under the protection of the blood of Jesus. In Christ we are delivered from the power of the darkness, the blessing is back with a vengeance against the enemy.

Get full understanding of who you are over the devil

The devil no longer has any right to hold us captive because man in Christ is under the umbrella of the BLESSING Genesis 1:28, Genesis 12:2-3, Genesis 9:7. Paul said to young Timothy *"meditate upon the things so that this profiting could appear"*. Meditate upon these things; give thyself wholly unto them, that thy profiting may appear to all. 1 Timothy 4:15 Paul said "consider what I say and the Lord will give the understanding in all things".

The Holy Spirit said in Proverbs 4: "in all thy getting get understanding". Because we do not meditate on these things we fail to grasp the reality of who we are and what truly belongs to us in God's plan of redemption. See your self redeemed by the blood of Jesus in the name of Jesus.

The bible states that we are sons of God now, not only in the sweet by and by but now while we are in this world. Remember that Jesus is the Son of God and he was in this world, born into this world. For God so loved the world that He gave His only begotten Son that whosoever believeth on Him, should not perish but have everlasting life. This everlasting life is the nature being, and substance of the living God St John 3:16.

Jesus did not come to hurt man but to restore him back to His Genesis 1:26 position with God. He humbled himself even unto death to make sure that we could get back what is truly ours before the foundation of the world. Remember Jesus is the lamb slain from the foundation of the world Eph 2:10 explains that we are the workmanship of God ordained by God to do good before time began. Solomon said "that which hath been is now". What God had planned before the world began found their fulfilment in the man called Jesus Christ, the anointing one and His anointing.

The head of the enemy was crushed 2000 years ago so that God could get us back into His family. We are back on the plan of God, we are in, we are His and He is ours. We are one in Christ Jesus. We are the body of Christ Jesus, the Son of the living God. We are the light of the world, because we are the children of light, we are in Him and He is in us. What a mighty God we serve. **I see this revelation producing powerful miracles in your life in the name of Jesus Christ.**

And because ye are sons, God has sent forth the Spirit of His Son into your hearts crying Abba Father. Therefore thou art, no more, a servant, but a son, and if a son, then an heir of God through Christ Galatians 4:6-7.

When I first came upon Galatians4:6-7, I was shocked. Friends the only reason why you have been given the Holy Spirit is because you are a son of God now. This has nothing to do with how we feel at times.

CHAPTER 5

WE ARE PART OF HIS PLAN FOR THESE END TIMES

For I know the plans I have for you saith the Lord Jeremiah 29:11.

Mk 16:15-20 "And he said unto them, Go ye into all, the world, and preach the gospel to every creature. He that believeth and is baptised shall be saved but he that believeth not shall be damned. And these signs shall follow them that believe. In my name shall they cast out devils; they shall speak with new tongues; they shall take up serpents and if they drink any deadly thing it shall not hurt them; they shall lay hands on the sick and they shall recover. So then after the Lord had spoken unto them, he was received up into heaven and sat on the right hand of God. And they went forth and preached every where the Lord working with them and confirming the word with signs following".

You are a spirit born of God and sustained by God; see this in your spirit. Ye are of God little children and have over come them 1 John 4:4. If you are born of God it means that you are in His likeness, we are just like Him on the inside. You are His kind. Remember the law of Genesis is that like begat like. You are a new creature that the world has never seen before 2 Corinthians 5:17. You are not of the world you are of God. You are of God. You are of God. 1 John 4:4.

You are the body of Christ 1 Corinthians 12:27.

As Jesus is now at the right hand of God so are you in this world for you are the body of Christ. This is what the devil does not want us to know. Satan has a blinding ministry so you don't know this. You have to meditate on this till light comes, but it will come if you stay with it day and night Joshua 1:8. Don't give up stay with it night and day.

You are the descendant of the Most High God. If we are like Him then we must have His potential in us. Yes you have His miracle ability in you. We can operate just like Him because as He is, so are we in this world. Jesus operated as a man without the limitations of this world. Jesus said that all things are possible to him that believeth Mk 9:23. He also said; *nothing shall* be impossible unto us, nothing Matt 17:20. He was using the faith law of Genesis 1 and Mark 11:23.

This is how He operated all His life on earth and always got astounding results, the trees obeyed Him, the wind obeyed Him, and even the devils obeyed Him. All sicknesses obeyed as He used the Genesis law of faith to get what He wanted. God pre-program every thing to obey the voice of faith ion the mouth of any believer. God wants us to stop walking by circumstances he wants us to stop living by what we see in this world. He wants us to understand that all our needs are already fully met in Christ Jesus our Lord. The time has come to take responsibility and just grow up in the Lord for the time is so short.

We can do the same because He said we can, and we can do what God said we can do. The people said we have never seen it of this kind. We can operate just like Jesus did in His Earth walk. If this is true which it is, it brings us on the same level like Jesus. We have failed to understand that we are the body of Christ on earth today. With His mighty spirit within us now, it will help us to do the works of Jesus Christ. We can crush the enemy with the weapons of God 2 Corinthians 10:1-3. We have the mighty name of Jesus to use against the enemy who comes to steal, kill and destroy. We are far from satanic oppression.

Man was created by God and given full Godlike responsibilities over the whole planet. Think about that for a moment Genesis 1:28 "And God blessed them and said to be fruit-full and multiply, replenish, subdue and take dominion". God said "Let them Rule!" Don't blame God for the mess you are in.

No limitations; God said "let them Rule" Gen 1:26.

God said "let man rule" so we are over anything the devil brings. How do we rule? We rule <u>with the word of God in our mouths</u>. We say what God says abut us no matter what we see before us. No matter what storms we face we can face them with all powerful words of God in our mouth. Remember you are the descendant of The Most High God; you are after His kind you can operate with faith like Him. No limitations were placed by God upon the man as long as he obeyed God.

The Church must learn to rule over the earth just like Jesus and the early Church. There is no limit placed by God on us, we can take back all that Satan and his cohorts have stolen from us. This is our time to rise over all traditions and act like sons of God on the earth. The time has come for us to be bold and daring like Caleb and Joshua.

The only thing that can break our connection is sin. Stay away from sin it is not worth it, so don't do it. Man lost control on the earth when he sinned against God. Solomon said that sin was a reproach to any nation/people. Man empowered the enemy when he obeyed Satan. Disobedience is a very dangerous thing, it is worst than witchcraft.

Adam stopped living by the word and started to live by flesh. We need to understand that to abandon God's word releases death upon us. Only the word can keep death away. The word of God is the highway of life it is the way to success all the blessings of the father. Therefore no matter what you are going through hold onto the word of the living God. You are an offspring of God so walk like one.

Paul said that we must walk worthy o this great call of God on our lives. The world system has failed, it is not working and many are dying. But, but in asking, ask, "Who will go for me" Isaiah 6:8 in the commission of Isaiah the question was who shall I send and who will go for us?" Will you go?

Rise to the level of the God kind of Life within and let us take the nations for Jesus Christ. You are who God says you are, you carry His life and power in you now. The Holy Spirit has hidden Purpose and Destiny in you. You are the descendant of the living God. You are not of this world, as He is Godly so are you on this planet. You are the seed of Abraham you are blessed with faith; you are full of Abraham's promise if you are born again Gal 3:29. You are blessed like the sons of Abraham.

Your job is to help the world with what you are carrying in you. This is your time so let's get moving with the Holy Spirit, into purpose and destiny.

Genesis Chapter 1 is full of the light and the wisdom of God; it is one of the most informative portions of the word of God. God is revealed as the creator of the heaven and the earth. Absolutely no help was given to him. He is the only one to bring order out of the chaos. Such was the state of the earth after the fall of Lucifer in which the universe was damaged in angelic warfare.

The greatest demonstration of God's power is put on display in Genesis Chapter 1. The ability of God to call light out of darkness has been revealed. You need to understand that you can operate the same way as your father because you are carrying the same creative power within you. It is not you, but what you are carrying in you. You are carrying the power that is not of this world but the power of the world to come. Jesus calls it resurrection power.

As a descendant of God you have the power to bind and loose. Peter wielded this power in Acts 3 and the blind man was healed. You notice he was so sure of the power that he took the man and helped him up. The man had never walked in his life but something from the next world was on Peter. This was the same man that had let the Lord down a few days before. Always remember that you wield this power by faith in the word of God. You stand on the word of promise like Abraham no matter what you see or feel in the natural. You know what God says is the answer, so you do not back off for anyone. You demand your God given rights as a son of God.

Faith cometh by hearing, hearing by the word of God faith comes by report.

You know that you are an heir of God. A joint heir with Christ. You see these things are real but in our hearts we have not received the light on them, but when we do, no weapon that is formed against us shall prosper.

Before God made the world He had it all in His heart; but to get it out He had to speak it out, He had to voice it out. You are designed the same way you must train yourself to say what you want, not what you see around you daily. If you want your life to be better say by faith what God has said to you in His word. Remember faith cometh by hearing and hearing the word of God which is the word of faith. This word must get into your mouth to get into your heart daily. OK, so God had all things in Him and when He was ready, He spoke out of Himself into the darkness that was upon the earth. When He spoke the Holy Spirit went to work with His creative ability in the word. You see it is the word that is creative not us but the word.

Believing, confessing and appropriating Abraham's Blessing which are yours in Christ. All that god gave to Abraham belongs to the believer now. All things were made by the genius creative ability in the spoken word of God. God said let there be light, and the light burst forth out of His inner most being. All things were created by the word of His mouth. As His son you have the same thing in you 2 Corinthians 4:13. We having the same spirit of faith therefore we believe and therefore speak. What do we_speak? We speak the promise to our situation no matter how it looks.

Using only what God says about us all the time will activate His power in our lives. We call the un-manifested to remove the manifested things we do not want. We speak only what God says about us, nothing else. Psalms 33:6 "By the word of the Lord were the heavens made and all the host of them, by the breath of His mouth Genesis1:1-28.

Things seen and things invisible were all created by the word of God at the dawning of time Col 1, by the time Adam came on the scene, on the sixth day all things were already in place. Finally God said that He wanted His kind to rule the Earth, so he made man to be in control of what He had created. You are the descendant of The Most High God. You are not from down here you are of the Super-ace, you are like God on the inside of you. The Super God is your Father.

You are no more a servant but a son.

Galatians 4:5-6 because you are sons, God has sent forth the spirit of His Son into your heart crying Abba Father. You are no more a servant but a son. Also, you are an heir of God. Wow!

Born again people are the descendants of The Most High God, we are like Him in our spirits Genesis 1:27. We were created out of what God is, which is His word we are an expressed image of God, offspring's, sons and family. We are in the divine family, so stop trying to get in. You are in by the blood of Jesus. The blood of Jesus has set us free and we are a redeemed people. Paul said "Stand fast in the liberty wherewith Christ has set us free" Galatians 5:1. Don't let the devil blind you, stand fast in your liberty with Christ. The New Testament speaks of the family in heaven and on earth. Remember who you are at all times.

You are the descendant of God Remember what the word says you are. Ye are of God little children and have overcome them, because greater is He that is in you than he that is in the world. Man that is born again is in the very image and likeness of God Himself.

You are the light of the world we are not of the darkness, all the mess in the world is not for us we can live far above it. Primarily we are in the Kingdom of God and not of the world system, which is so weak and full of death and decay. You carry what God is in you all the time, do not go by how you feel, walk by faith all the time practicing faith all the time, and speaking the word at all times. You are the descendants of the Living God.

CHAPTER 6

BECAUSE WE ARE SONS

Because we are sons of God he had sent forth the spirit of His Son into our hearts Gal 4:5-6. Your heart is your spirit. Your heart is you. Your heart is the real you. You are a divine being. God has given us his very own life as his son Jesus Christ this mean we have divine status in Christ. Ye are not of the world but ye are of God. You are a spirit with the Holy Spirit within. Your spirit is far superior to your soul. Your body has a soul but you are first a spirit in the image and likeness of God himself.

This revelation is very important to getting to know the Lords will for your life. It's because we are sons, is the reason why God is working all things out for our good. No matter what you are going through it will not destroy you for God is with you and for you. The enemy is always trying to destroy the people of God but he cannot do it because we have protection from above. Isa 54:17.

> The manifestation of the sons of God is
> here now we are taking our place.

You are a son now you are in the divine family at the expense of Christ, we are not talking about when you die. We are what we are now in Christ Jesus. We are the very heart of God's holy family, chosen in Christ Jesus the son of God. We are citizens of the new world that is to come. We have access to the things of the next world now because we are from there in the spirit. Spirits are not from this world this world is a natural world it cannot produce a spirit. We were created in Christ who is a spirit who is the word of God so we are what the word says we are.

THE DESCENDANTS OF GOD

We are the new born again race of beings subject only to the Most High God. We are not of this world but we are chosen out of it to walk with God forever. We are spirit not flesh we only live in the flesh but we are really spirit just like our father who is Spirit. This is why the word says we must walk worthy of this great calling of the Lord on our lives. God will never allow his family to perish. God so love the world that he gave his only Son that we might have eternal life John 3:16. He has invested himself into his family and we are his eternal seed inheritance out of this world. We are his portion forever. David said the Lord is the portion of my inheritance. We are the people of God a peculiar people.

Nothing is impossible for the people of God when we stand on the word of the living God. The bible said that the people that do know their God shall be strong and do exploits. Dan 11:32. Man in Christ will never be left alone because we have the Holy Spirit with us all the time. God told us I will never leave thee nor forsake thee. God said I will not fail thee so, be strong in the Lord your God and in the power of His might and be of good courage. Eph 6:10.

Mark 16:15-20 is about man taking his place of dominion in Christ Jesus our Lord.

We must learn to operate in kingdom power and dominion in Christ Jesus. Gen 1:28 and Mark 16:15-20 is really the same thing talking about taking dominion over the enemy. Yes the scriptures make it very clear that we have total dominion power over Satan the enemy of the kingdom of God. This dominion power must be exercise daily for it to work for us in the invisible world and the natural world. You are a descendant of the living God. Rom 8:14 for as many as are led by the spirit of God they are the sons of God. This is talking about us in Christ Jesus. Did you know that God has given us joint seating in heavenly places in Christ Jesus? Eph 2:1-6 study.

And God blessed them, and God said unto them, "Be fruit-full, and multiply, and replenish the earth, and subdue it and have dominion over the fish of the sea, and over the fowl of the air and over every living things that moveth upon the earth" Genesis 1:28 and he said unto them, "Go ye into all the world and preach the gospel to every creature. He that believeth and is baptised shall be saved but he that believeth not shall be damned".

And these signs shall follow them that believe, In my name shall they cast out devils, they shall speak with new tongues, they shall take up serpents and it shall not harm them and if they drink any deadly thing it shall not hurt them, they shall lay hands on the sick and they shall recover" Mk 16:15. So then after the Lord had spoken unto them, he was received up into heaven and sat at the right hand of God. And they went forth and preach every where the Lord confirming the word signs following Mk 16:15-20. You are for signs and wonders because you carry the glory of the Lord inside of you.

These words in Mark 16 give us details as to what we are and how we are to operate in this world. The enemy has been working hard to get our focus off the divine mandate that the Lord has given us. I see you operating on a daily basis. Your time of obscurity is over. You will now excel in the name of Jesus. You are a winner; you will rise above all the storms in the name of Jesus. You are a winner you are made of the word. The word is the winner and so are you in this world. Yu are a supernatural being because you have the spirit of God on the inside of you forever, you will never, never be separated from the Lord again. <u>He is your</u> father and you are His child. You have the divine right to win all the time. You are the descendant of God.

> You are a spirit this is what you really are.

When you were born again you became an immortal spirit being, you have eternal life in you as a gift from God Rom 6:23. 1 John 5:12 & 13 "He that hath the son hath life" = Zoe. The spirit of man is the candle of the Lord searching all the inward parts of the belly Proverbs 20:27. Friend get this into your spirit once and for all. You are a spirit being just like God Gen 1:27. You are a God like being. Divine power, divine potential are hidden within you right now. God has hidden gifts in you that can make you to be an asset to your generation. You were born into the world at the right time; you are at the right place for a miracle. You are a son of God and Jesus is your Lord and master.

Job 32 "You are an eternal spirit and you will always be. **There is a spirit in man.**

God will talk to you from within your inner man not the flesh man. You are spirit with God's life nature and power in you now. All you need now is inside of you. God operates from inside of you. You have to know this in your heart always. You are his descendant.

Most of us are looking far too much on the external to get answers from the Lord. We all need to walk by faith in the Word of God. If it is by faith this really mean it is already done. For the word says we are walking by faith not by sight. Sons of God are really heirs of the living God and this mean that one day the Lord will come again. Please keep you eyes on the master and he will take make to.

Please remember Jesus said the Comforter will be in you and with you so we are a God indwelt people full of divine power to help others. Now we all need to become more conscious of this in our hearts and we do this by meditating the word very often as a life style. I believe this is the problem we do not set aside proper time to get the word into our hearts. To become the man God talks about is Psalms 1 we need to engraft the sayings of Jesus into our hearts then, we need to do them regardless of the external things we see around us. This is what Jesus was so good at, in spite of the things he saw in the natural he did not let them stop him from doing what the Father wanted him to do.

Meditate on the word until you get the right attitude. God's words when meditated on will produce miracle mentality in us. Your spirit is designed by God to grow the promises of God within. We are first of all spirit. It is with your spirit that you touch God with your faith. We having the same spirit of faith, according as it is written, I believed and therefore have I spoken; we also believe and therefore speak 2 Corinthians 4:13.

Your body cannot touch God only your spirit of faith. God has given you faith in your heart and in His word so that you can get back in touch with him at anytime Romans 12:3, Ephesians 2:8. Because you are spirit born of the spirit of God it is impossible to know yourself without knowing God, without having a relationship with Him. It is as we get to know Him in our spirit we find fulfilment, satisfaction, destiny, purpose and the reason for living.

Purpose and destiny will come alive as we spend time fellowshipping with the Lord in our spirit in the word. There is no greater blessing in this life than having God in the spirit of man. It is the greatest union in the universe. Nothing is more important than this. This is what Adam lost. He lost the indwelling presence of the Lord that was in him. He lost the glory of God that was inherent within. He lost the abilities and attributes of God that was within him. He lost the righteousness of God that was in him.

He lost the peace of God. The glory was gone when he sinned, wisdom abandoned him, but God's grace and mercy didn't. God began to speak about the seed of the woman that would bruise the head of the serpent Genesis 3:15. Jesus brought it all back to us in the new birth. We are now the manifested sons of the Lord God on the earth. This is your time of manifestation so enjoy your self as you do the word daily like Jesus.

You are in His image and likeness. You are a spirit. You are not in a natural battle, but an invisible spiritual war. Satan is your real constant enemy. There is a battle raging over your life on earth, in terms of how you should live it. God want you to live it His way. Satan wants you to live it his way. Because you are a spirit the problem you face in life must be spiritual. Most times in life we need to get our eyes off the natural and look to God our father by faith. For we walk by faith not by sight 2 Corinthians 5:7.

The devil wants us to stay ignorant of the spiritual things that rightfully belongs to us, he does not want us to know our potential or who we really are in Christ Jesus Hosea 4:6 My people are destroyed for lack of knowledge.

My people are destroyed for lack of knowledge. Lack of knowledge is a killer. All of us need to be growing in the things of the spirit. Your spirit has the ability to grow up in the things of God Eph 4.The time has come for radical changes in how we see ourselves. We must learn to embrace what God says about us, not what people or the world is saying. What God says is eternal reality. What God says is the truth. What God says is the answer.

Learn to see yourself in Christ. Take your eyes off the things that are seen and focus on the unseen things of the spirit. If ye then be raised in Christ, seek those things which are above where Christ sitteth on the right hand of God Col 3:1

You are a spirit so focus on the things of the spirit. To be carnally minded is death. To think like the world is death. To think like God is life and peace in the Holy Ghost. Everything that the devil is involved in, leads to death, and destruction. Everything that God is involved in leads to life eternal. God brings light; the devil brings death pain and destruction.

The spirit of man is the candle of the Lord. This means that whatever God is going to do through you, will be done in your spirit and through your spirit man. Remember that the greater one who is the Holy Spirit is constantly living in you. You are always anointed because he lives within you. Be, God inside minded and the miraculous will become normal for you. You are not a body; you are a spirit with the life of God in you. You are over the devil not under him. You have the power to crush him under your feet.

The fruits of the spirit are spiritual forces in you

There is a spirit in man and the inspiration of the Almighty giveth understanding Job 32:8. All the fruits of the spirit come out of your spirit by the Holy Spirit in you. All the gifts of the spirit, flows from the recreated spirit of the new creature. You are the duplicate of God in His image and likeness, you are a spirit being; without any form of condemnation in Christ Jesus. God himself has birth you out of Himself for such a time as this. Rom 8:1. You are not an accident, God made you out of Himself 1Peter 1:23.

There is purpose and destiny hidden within you by the Lord. God love you because you are a part of Him. He will never leave you or forsake you. Always remember that you are a partaker of God's divine nature 2 Peter 1:1-4. When you were born again (recreation, you were recreated) with the special Zoë life of God in you. You literally passed out, from death into life John 5:24. You are now the very recipient of eternal life the very life of God Himself. Jesus said if a man keeps my saying he shall never see death John 8:51.

The devil does not want you to know this. God said be fruit-full, multiply, replenish, subdue and have dominion. Please remember that God said these things after He empowered us with 'the Blessing'. The bible says, "And God blessed them" and the said word were spoken over us by God from Genesis and God has never changed His mind about His plan and purpose for our lives upon the earth.

Release the fruit-fullness that is within you. The fruit-fullness that is within you needs Meditation which will produce motivation. Motivation will produce action. Action on the word will produce results. Remember Jeremiah 7:23 "Obey my voice and I will be your God". We obey by doing and giving voice to the word.

A special race of spirit beings

Friend you are a part of God's special race of divine family. You have been given divine status in the new birth and by the rights of the blood covenant. The word says you are a partaker of the Lord's Table. You have arrived because God is now your Father, your power, your ability. There is no longer any restraint. All things are now possible because God is on your side. Romans 8:32, if God be for us, who can be against us.

On the inside God has made you more than a conqueror just like Jesus. You have the power to multiply, replenish, and subdue. You have dominion. This is not for 'in the sweet by and by'. In the sweet by and by there will be no enemies to subdue. However, in this world we are surrounded by enemies of our spirit, soul and body. The time has come for us to understand who we are in Christ Jesus.

Jesus said that He was in the Father and the Father was in Him and we are in Him. See Jesus on the inside of you now. You are not just natural you are a supernatural being, in the image and likeness of God. Genesis 1:27 "God is a spirit and they that worship Him must worship in spirit and in truth". Worship speaks of intimacy with God. To be honest what God wants from us is true worship. The true worship brings us on the same level with God; God is seeking for true worshippers, not preachers, but worshipers. As we learn to worship then we find our true purpose. Purpose and destiny will be revealed when we learn to spend time in His presence. I see you as a true in the nature of Jesus. Because you are a spirit being just like God but created by Him, born out of Him, you now have the capacity to operate on the same level just like God.

The greatest part of man is his spirit nature that he got from the father of spirits. Hebrews 12 "like begets like". This is law that cannot be revised by anyone. We birth out by the word of God. We are what we are in the word of God, regardless of what is going on around us and this is still the unchanging truth of God's word.

The time has come to think and operate as the spiritual being that we are in Christ Jesus. It is as we embrace what we are on the inside that the Holy Spirit will do His mighty work through us. The body of Christ needs to wake up and let God have his way in the body of Christ.

Every detail of our life is under divine scrutiny because we are sons not slaves. We can touch God with our spirit by acting on the word of God that we believe. We are not just human beings. We are spirit beings with the incorruptible nature of God on the inside of us all the time. From the moment we got born again we became what God says we are.

God is on the inside. For we are greater on the inside than we are on the outside; but the enemy wants you to focus on the outside. That way you will never truly know who you are in Christ.

Remember Jesus dwells in your hearts by faith, not by sight, or by feelings. Feelings change but the word of God in your heart and in your mouth cannot change. It is impossible for God to change. Jesus said nothing shall be impossible for us, but His will only work when we take our stand on the word of God. You see when you know that God cannot lie, or change or fail; it gives us great faith to obtain the promises of God. Most times on the outside what God have said looks impossible, but we must remember that if He said it, to Him it is already done therefore we need to see things how he said it in his word to us.Dont focus on the seen.

The fight of faith is to believe him, in our hearts that it is already done by Him. We must believe what He believes and say it, to get what He can do. Everything that God told Abraham seemed impossible, but the God that we serve knows no limit.

This is some thing we must learn to receive in our hearts that God will do what he says he will do no matter how it seems impossible he will still bring his word to us to pass in process of time. We can as spirit beings develop the miracle mentality of God.

But it takes time to get the word into us. We have been conned by the devil for so long some times to see what God is saying does take quite a while. God's word is full of Himself, and He knows no limit at all. The same is true for those of us in Christ Jesus. Be fruit-full, multiply, replenish, subdue and have dominion. Now that is real power. You are the **descendant** of The Most High God! This is your time for to manifest the power of the Lord to the nations of the world. Go demonstrate the power of the Lord that is laying latent within you in the name of Jesus. As a son of God this, really mean that you are subject of his worthy kingdom blessing which is eternal life the nature of the living God. There is nothing better in this world like eternal life. It is the immortal life of God given to man by God when we receive Christ.

CHAPTER 7

WHAT THE BELIEVER IN CHRIST IS

Jesus said, "They are not of the world even as I am not of the world" John 17:16 they are not of the world, Even as I am not of the world. What a statement! Read on, He that is joined unto the Lord is one spirit 1Corinthians 6:17. The believer is much more than a natural being we are not what the world say but what God say about us in his world. We are not to be controlled by anything in the natural. The world calls us Christians but we are not Christians but we are in fact sons of the living God that have never existed before.

We are the very own sons of God himself in Christ Jesus the Lord. On the inside we are new on the inside all the time. You are called by God a son and a new kingdom has taken hold of you. You are the head and not the tail. This is what we are now in him a son of the light kingdom. Yes "The light domain", which is God's domain. This is all in you in the new birth.

In all these things we are more than conquerors Romans 8:31-32.

The law of the spirit of life in Christ Jesus is in us now. We are not of the night but of the light. This is what Jesus gave back to us in the new birth. We are not of the night or of darkness. We are the people of the light. God's light.

The Lord have made it very clear that his people is not from down here we are from the God Race; we are born of the Most High God we are

Descendants of the living God. This is clear in the word of God. You can go to church sing in the choir preach give offerings yet you are not born again. The only way into the kingdom of Jesus is to be born again by the spirit of the living God Rom 10:9-10. This is not a natural birth it is a supernatural one within your inner man. Therefore this is not something that man can do it is a supernatural work of the word of God when we believe and confess Jesus as the Lord of our lives. What we have is not religion but Christ on the inside. The believer is complete in the Lord. We are fully born again we fully belong to Jesus.

Look at this remarkable scripture below in 1 Peter 1:23

It is very important for you to understand who you are in Christ and you can only find this out in the word of God.

Being born again not of corruptible seed but of incorruptible by the Word of God which liveth and abideth forever. 1 Peter 1:23. Jesus also said ye must be born again. Ok, so you see that, your spirit was not born of natural sperm but of the word of God, so the Word of God was the seed that made you in Christ Jesus. We are His workmanship created in Christ Jesus Eph 2:10. Therefore we are not from the Earth but heaven itself. See and know in your spirit that in Christ you are 100% complete by the blood of Christ Jesus. Col 2:10.

The believer in Christ is not of this world the believer is a new spiritual being created in Christ Jesus by the word of God. We are born of God himself so; we are what God we are. One of the major problems we have in the body of Christ is we have not embraced the above scripture the way we should.

Many of us are still living and walking by sight, living to please the flesh only. 2 Corinthians. 5:7. But God wants us to live by faith in his promises. For we walk by faith and not by sight, not how we feel but by faith. We are still holding back on our faith and striving to fit into the world system of the Devil. We are still, believing the lies Satan told us over the years but Jesus said *"we are not of the world"* John 17:16. Therefore we are what God says we are in his word. Start calling yourself what God calls you in his eternal word.

It is not right for the Church to live as the people of the world do, we aught to copy Christ every day. We must become imitators of the living God we must become God's followers in this world. We must stop thinking in our man made boxes and live by God's word daily. We must walk as Jesus walked in his earth walk by faith. He that saith he abideth, in him, ought himself also to walk even as he walked 1 John 2:6.

As sons of God, we are born of God not, the Devil or his evil nature we are partakers of, the very nature of the living God, this is what we are. The very nature of God is within us right now. We are partakers/sharers of divine nature 2 Peter 1:1-4. The word also says we are born again not of corruptible seed 1 Peter 1:23.Which means we are the seed of God in the earth today because; God's seed is the only incorruptible seed. The seed that produced us is the very word of God himself and we know that the word is God so the believer is connected to God by his word. Look, it is so clear we have to be stupid to miss it. We are not of corruptible seed so if this is so, the rest of the verse is also true because it says we are of incorruptible seed which is the word of God which liveth, and abideth forever 1 Peter_1.23. This is truly what we are in Christ Jesus our Lord this is all at his expense yes; this is what is available by his grace to all mankind.

You need to truly see who you are in Christ in the word and, accept yourself as God has created you perfect in Christ Jesus. In him you are perfect and complete. Col 2:10 All good things about you is about who and what you are in Christ Jesus and the word explains what you are so dig into the word until light comes to you. Jesus said search the scriptures. That was what he did in his earth walk. Luke. 4:18-20 Jesus spoke very often what he saw in the word about himself and so should you. In the Torah God said over 25 hundred times 'I AM_the Lord'. So start saying what, he said about you.

There is no good within man but from above. Every good thing in us was given to us. Now, we know that the testimony of the Lord is sure. Psalms 19:7. Yes God's word is his testimony to every generation, and no one can change God's testimony which is his covenant word with us. His word is really the proof of what we really are in Christ his word is the evidence of what he made us in Christ. If God say's we are born again of his <u>seed</u> then we are, what he say's we are. We may not understand it but because God cannot lie what he says is always the truth. We are what he say's we are, we are born again of him we are his seed on earth we are, his Representative.

We are His witnesses to this generation.

Acts 1:8, "Ye shall be witnesses unto me into all the world". The work of the body of Christ is to re-present Jesus to the world. The believer is a direct witness of the almighty God and we are brothers and sisters to Jesus himself we are God's sons of light right now on the earth. We are the blood brothers of Christ Jesus. We are beings that have never existed before. In the new birth God has wiped out our old way of sinful life. He did this with the blood of Jesus in the believer. To God, it is as though, we had never sinned he sees us as his righteousness on the earth. In Jesus Christ the believer is perfect and accepted in the beloved Ephesians 1. In Christ we have been promoted to divine status in heavenly places in Christ Jesus Ephesians 1; 3. This is why the word says we are Joint-heirs with Jesus Christ. Romans 8:16. Think about what it means to be a joint-heir. What does Jesus own? Because whatever Jesus owns we own it as well, believers are co-owners and co sharers by blood covenant rights. This is what he has done not us, but him. So give him all the praise always.

Now you need to understand that this is a reality in your inner man all the time whether you feel like it or not it is still so in the realms of the spirit. Yes this is the genius of real Christianity. Man in Christ is a new creature; man in Christ is a divine being with God's life on the inside. Real Christianity is about sons of God on the earth today operating in the power of Jesus Christ. John 14:12. Jesus said, the works that I do shall ye do also. We are capable of operating just like Jesus in his earth walk. As he is so are we 1 John 4:17. This is about God taking his rightful place back in the hearts of man. Col. 1:27 Christ in you the hope of glory Colossians 1:27, yes this is the miracle of what we have in us and it is the best, this is not religion this is God in man. What we are in Christ is clearly revealed in the word of God.

The God that opened the Red sea for his people is living in you right now. Learn to see this and accept it by faith. **Christ dwells in your heart by faith** Ephesians 3:17. So we see here that the Christ the anointed one is living within the believer thus making the believer his dwelling place. God makes the believer his eternal home, both on earth and in heaven later, when we leave this world by death or the rapture. We are h very temple of God himself this is what we are here on the earth. Ye are the temple of the Living God 1 Corinthians 6.

This is the greatest miracle in the universe that sinners can become sons of God on the earth. Ye are sons Galatians 4:5-7. As many as received him he gave us power to become sons of God John 1:12. The purpose of Jesus coming to the earth was to rise up a kingdom of sons of the living God. He came to give back the life of God to sons that were dead in sins and trespasses.

Understand that when Adam fell we all fell with him from the life realms to the death and darkness realms. So Jesus had to take up the role of redeemer as the second Adam bringing us back to God with his shed blood.

You can live the life of faith just like Jesus if you focus on all you are in him embracing what you are in him and all this, at the expense of the Lord Jesus. Philippians 4:13.

No matter what we face in this world we can be confident that we have already won in Christ Jesus. The Devil is a liar. In Christ we are all winners God don't make failures.

What are we?

We are God's very own seed in the world we are in his image and we are in his likeness in the world right now. Gen 1:28 is still in force Today God has never change his will for us on earth. Be blessed be fruitful replenish subdue and have dominion. God has never change his plan for man, the mandate is still the same. You were created for Greatness by the Lord himself. For I know the Plans I have for you saith the Lord, plans to prosper you and give you an expected end. Jeremiah 29:11.

This is why he has placed the Blessing on you. *Psalms 3:8 "thy Blessing is upon thy people"* and Numbers 22:12 which says, "Curse not the people for they are "Blessed". The Blessing is the endowment power of God's might in our spirits as a believer. It is the support of God on man, it is the proof that God is with us. The blessing is the demonstrative ability of God on man called the anointing. It is the evidence that WE ARE NOT OF THIS WORLD SYSTEM. John 17:16. *They are not of the world Jesus said even as I am not of the world.* This power is given to us so we can do the impossible among men; it is given to attract men to Jesus Christ and to meet the needs of man to bring glory to God.

It is the divine power on man for service to the king. The blessing of the Lord is fully on the believer all the time but we need to be aware of it all the time. Thy blessing is upon thy people. Psalms 3:8. We have what God's word says we have. The blessing makes it clear to the powers of hell that we belong to the order of the living God not the order of this natural world.

We are what God says we are which have nothing to do with how we feel at times, what God says is still the truth and we must never lie against the truth. James. 3. What are we? We are God's eternal sons on the earth today. Our purpose is to demonstrate Jesus to a dying world & show forth the praises of the living God who has called us out of darkness into his marvellous light. We are God's Kings and priests on the earth. Therefore we should be reigning over the earth. We are a kingdom of priest and kings on the earth. Rev 1:5. Unto God and, Jesus is our Lord and master, not the devil.

We are no longer under the curse of the LAW but under the Blessing of Abraham. Understand that when you were born again God made you brand new on the inside within the inner man. If any man be in Christ he is a new creature all things are become new and old things are pass away 2 Corinthians. 5:17. You are really a spirit with the life, nature of God himself within you. All is new on the inside right now. He that hath the Son hath life and this life is God's own life 1 John 5:11-12. God's miracle working life is working right there within you. It is eternal life.

The creator God has made you his eternal home so you will never be away from him because he lives in you. This is what Jesus came to give back to man this is your rightful place with God this is what you are. Yes; you are in his family you are his. When you truly accept the above and say it daily you will see things start to change for you big time. You see, believing it is not enough you must learn to think this way and say it out of your mouth so you can become aware of it in your spirit man daily.

This way of word of God thinking must become a daily thing with you in order to get it to work in you all the time no matter what is going on around you, learn to think this way. You see, this way of thinking God's word and talking God's word will cause the power of the Lord to flow out of you and effect changes in your life and circumstances. This is also how you put your many angels to work for you, by speaking the word of God daily as a lifestyle. This is what is lacking in the body of Christ, yes we are still thinking and talking like the world does.

This is why we need to change the way we think big time and move over to word of God thinking and talking and praying. Proverbs 21:7 as a man thinks in his heart spirit, so is he. This is why we must be careful what we are thinking about and watch what we are saying all the time.

Again what is the believer?

Ye are of God little children 1 John 4:4 Yes this is what you are on the inside right now.

In our spirit we are not of our family down here, we are of God, we are from the next world. Ye are of God little children. God himself is our father through Jesus Christ the son of the living God. As sons we are empowered with the BLESSING of the Lord. Genesis 1:28. The Blessing is on us right now as sons of God. Behold I give you power over all the power of the enemy and nothing shall by any means hurt you. Luke 10:19. We are covered God.

If God say's we are of him how dare anyone say, we are not. But this is how the devil works he comes to try to mess up our identity of who we are in Christ and, he does it with words and, bad circumstances. So when things go wrong he tell us we are not what the bible says we are, he tries to get us to focus on the seen and, not the unseen which is how we must live. We were created to live by the unseen 2 Corinthians 5:7. We are a faith people this is what we are. Paul said "the just shall live by faith".

As a recreated spirit in Christ you have to learn to live by what you are made up of which is the word of the great father God. This is why we need to confess daily that, we are what God say we are and I do this no matter what is going on in our lives or ministry.

If you want God to change things for you will have to learn to copy him daily, this is what you are doing when you confess the word of God out loud.

Learn to live out of your inner man where the Holy Spirit is living learn to talk like him and do this very often daily. Make special time to spend with Him often and He will show you great and mighty things you don't know now. Ye are of God, what a statement, what a reality in the realms of God almighty. You came out of God in Christ in your inner man. This is who you are, born from above are you in him. As he is so are we in this world. You are just like him on the inside. 1 John 4:17.

Jesus said we must be born from above John 3 and we are like the wind which no man can tell you where the wind is going we are like that on the inside. If we are like God then we can do the things that God say's we should do because WHATEVER HE COMMANDS US TO DO HE GIVES US THE POWER TO DO IT. So we are without excuse so rise up and do the word of God which is the power of God.

It will help your faith life much if you daily say what God say about you in his word. This is how your faith will grow in the things of God very fast and you will rise to the level of your confession. If you hear your own voice saying often what God says about you, your faith will grow very fast.

Your spirit and your soul and body will respond to the words you speak daily, that is why Jesus explains "Ye shall have whatever you say" Mark 11:23. Yes you shall have what you say. You are now in the kingdom because you said it and, God heard you and saved you. Satan could no longer hold you because you said it and God responded by saving you and placing you into the kingdom of Jesus Christ the son of God. Romans 10:9-10 Your, confession of faith in Christ got you into the kingdom. You were born again because of what you believed and said. Because with the heart man believeth unto, and with the mouth confession is made unto, this spiritual law will never change.

The believer is God's chosen vessel, full of God's Blessing power (Loaded with the Blessing) for success victory and deliverance. Jesus said in my name cast the Devil out. Why can we cast them out? It's because we are over them all in the realm of the spirit. Remember that you are a spirit with a soul living in a body but you are really spirit. Now, your spirit man is where you have divine connection with your father God who is a spirit. This is why we need to learn to listen to our inner man because it is there we will hear from God. This is an inner thing not a natural thing and it comes from God.

Now do you remember when Jesus said all power is given unto me in heaven and in earth? Yes? Ok well that same power is in you now as a son of God in your inner man. You have the same authority because Jesus gave you his authority and his power. Matthew 28. Luke 10:19. Acts 1:8. The time has come to get on with the work of the kingdom. You are **loaded** with the power of God so don't pray for power but pray as to learn how to operate it by faith in God's word.

As sons of God we have the right to re-present Jesus to man in the earth. Now the power of the Lord in the believer is unlimited. Mark 9:23, all things are possible to the believer because we believe and say what God says so God then does as we say. *God will do what you say if he said it before you*, wow that is powerful. You are always on the mind of God as sons and believer's because you have a covenant with him and covenant cannot be broken. My covenant will I not break nor alter the thing that is gone out of my lips. Psalms 89:34. You notice he said the thing is gone out of his lips? As covenant people of God we are under the umbrella of the Blessing. The blessing is the mark that we belong to God himself.

Your healing, and prosperity has already gone out of the mouth of God. Your success in life has gone out of the mouth of God. Take your portion. Psalms 89:34.

You are what he says you are. You have what he says you have you are blessed!

To be blessed by God means you are endowed with power from on high it means you have the power to rise above.

What is the believer in Christ?

We are citizens of the Kingdom of God himself Eph 2:19, which means that God is fully responsible for us which means, all our needs are already met in Christ!

This kingdom or domain is already within the believer all the time it is not out there some where it is within us here and now. We seem to think God is going to do it but he has already given us all things in Christ Jesus from before the world began the word says that which is to be done is already done. From the foundation of the world God met all our needs in Christ Jesus. We are the very seed of God in the earth realms representing the God of heaven. We are his colony on the earth so we are backed by him.

We have full rights in the kingdom just like any other citizens in heaven. We are, in warfare on the earth that is in rebellion against God so God supplies all our needs according to his riches in glory by Christ Jesus our Lord Philippians 4:19.

Including the armour of God for battle in the invisible world around us and in the battlefield of our minds where the enemy seems to attack a lot.

We are not on the Earth on our own but, the Holy Spirit himself is with us in this war we are in. Plus remember, we have already won in Christ Jesus. We are God's army on the earth today so the full Blessing package is with us all the time that is why God says we are loaded with his blessing benefits Psalms 68:19. If you are born again you are loaded with heavens best - the Blessing.

We are possessors of the very life of God himself. Yes you have passed from death to life in Christ Jesus. This was made available to us at the expense of Jesus going to the cross. The resurrection life of Jesus Christ is living in the believer all the time. This life we stir up by acting on the word of God all the time. We don't have to feel any thing all we need to do is just do the word which is anointed all the time. The word of God is Jesus himself he is the written and the living word of God. Remember God cannot, back away from his word ever he is in his word all the time. We must learn not to back away from the word of the Lord as well. The secret of true success in this life is to stand on the word of faith consistently.

Understand that the word will not work for you until you believe it and say it out of your mouth. Many are not receiving because; they are not saying continually what God has said about them in his word. However this is the way to get God to work for you, we have to say what he says about us in his word all the time.

Never let up on speaking what God say about you. Say you are born again very often. Say you are his child very often. Say you are rich very often. Say you can't be broke

Very, often and you will see God move for you as he does what you say out of your mouth. Decree daily how great God is in you and you will see him work in you.

You are the DESCENDANT OF THE MOST HIGH GOD. So you are not of the world you are of the Lord God. Jesus said "ye are not of the world even as I am not of the world John 17:16" so your identity is in Christ Jesus. When you are asked by the World who you are tell them you are born of God. Tell them your home is in heaven and you are just here to help them into the kingdom. Do not be afraid to sound out to others who you are in Christ, that is what Jesus and John the Baptist did they sounded out who they were in the word of God and heaven backed them fully. Tell them the Lord God is your real father and you have divine protection. Omnipotence is your mother and father.

You are a son you are a daughter you belong in the same class of being as your father-God. Take your place by the faith of God and operate in the kingdom from your divine status in Christ Jesus. You are not from down here you are of God himself so no power of the devil can defeat you in Christ Jesus. You are a success you are blessed Genesis 1:28.

You operate by the LAW of the Spirit of Life in Christ Jesus with faith-filled force-filled words. You are a world changer yes you bring change from heaven to the dead in the world. They need you more than how you need them so go help them with God's life and nature in you. They are perishing so move fast in the Lord and go help them into the kingdom of Jesus Christ.

This is what we are in Christ

For thou art a holy people unto the Lord thy God: the Lord thy God hath chosen thee to be a special people unto himself, above all people upon the face of the Earth Deut 7:6. In Christ Jesus we are very special to the Lord. We are his holy people! We are above all people and we are the head and never the tail. In Christ we are God's chosen people and our purpose is to serve Jesus Christ the son of the living God. God has a people that are in blood covenant with him.

Beloved now are we the sons of God and it doth not yet appear what we shall be but we know that we shall be like him for we shall see Him as He is 1 John 3:3 You are raised from the dead with Christ. Colossians 3:1-4 Jesus Christ is now your new life and you are hidden in Christ in God. All this took place before you were born but you received it when you received Christ as saviour and Lord. When you received Jesus the Blessing was placed on you by God the father. Jesus said the father himself loves you. You are called the redeemed because you have redemption in Christ. Ephesians 1:7.

You have this redemption by the blood of, Jesus Christ your Lord. This is why Paul taught that we can do all things through Christ which strengthens us. Phil 4:13. In Christ you are always anointed to succeed to prosper 100%. You do this by learning to think and talk like God does all the time. Just keep doing it daily day after day and it will grow in you. You will have to bring the word into you private life as well, not just your ministry life you will have to learn to live the word daily. James 1:22, be ye doers of the word and not hearers only. This is where many miss it by not speaking the word into the problems of life. They will say you are mad and you are showing off but you are doing what God say's do so keep speaking the word daily.

With our status in Christ we are now the righteousness of God in Christ on the earth right now this is what we are. This is what you are, and you are what God's word says you are no matter how you feel this cannot change. We are the children of the most High God the Descendants of the living God. We have been given power over all the power of the Devil in the demonic realm. Remember what we have been talking about. We are descendants of the living God. We lost our place with the fall of the first Adam but the second Adam Jesus Christ came and gave us back our place in God. This is a supernatural package that, encompass all of our life on earth and, our life in heaven in the future. So we are not weaklings as satan wants us to think because the mind of Jesus Christ which is MIRACLE thinking, is made available to all of us in the kingdom word of God. This is why Paul said in the word "Let this mind be in you which was also in Christ Jesus" Phil 2:5 so we need to learn to see things the way God said it in his word.

This takes time to develop it does not come over night but it is there for all of us if we will trust Gods word and take action based on what his word says to us and about us. Really we should live daily by all what God have said in his word yes this is the great fight of faith because Satan wants us to live by what we see going on around us and how we feel in our bodies. With God's word in our mouth we are more than a conqueror over the devil and his evil demons. Do not be afraid of the enemy for the Lord is your shepherd and he is by your side. You shall not want for protection even in the valley of the shadows of death but you have to open your mouth daily and declare what God says you are in him. You must say of the Lord what the word says about you Psalms 91.

The word declares whatsoever we bind on earth shall be bound in heaven and whatsoever we loose on the earth shall be loosed in heaven Matthew 18:18 this power is given by Jesus himself to the sons of the Living God. Matt 18:18-20. This is the same power that was in Jesus Christ that is given to us. The same power that was in the mouth of Adam before the fall and the same power that was in the mouth of all the prophets of old. It is power that was at work in the life of father Abraham and Sarah. As the sons of the Living God understand that we are co-possessors of heaven and earth Just as Abraham was in his day, Genesis 14.

You are a king in your spirit man so you must learn to give orders in the spirit to your angels that have been sent to minister for you and to you. Your inheritance in Christ is unlimited 100% this is why the word says all things are possible to us who believe the word. You are a co owner/sharer with Jesus Christ Rom 8:17.

Blessed be the God and father of our Lord Jesus Christ who hath blessed us with all spiritual blessings in heavenly places in Christ Jesus. Ephesians1:3. According to the above scripture God has given us all that he has for us in Christ yes in the realms of the invisible where God lives he has given us all in Jesus Christ. The word talks about the unsearchable riches of Christ so, what we have in us is totally without any form of limit. We are now in the realms where all things are possible. Jesus said "nothing shall be impossible unto you". Matt 17:20. It is the enemy that comes to put limit on us but Jesus came that we might live the abundant lifestyle of God John 10:10. We are blest above all other people on the earth because we have this great anointing Blessing on us as sons of the living God. ***Thy blessing is upon thy people***. Psalms 3:8 you are blessed beyond measure in the Lord because his blessing is on you right now by faith. You have the blessing.

Blessed be the God and father of our Lord Jesus Christ who hath blessed us with all spiritual blessings in heavenly places in Christ Jesus. This is reality. Meditate daily on the reality of your inheritance in Christ Jesus. Ephesians 1:7 you have been redeemed by his blood.

Study the book of Ephesians with much care and you will see what the Lord have done for you. You are a son right now but remember you have to grow up in him in all things. If you do not grow up in the things of the Word you will not be able to enjoy the benefits of your inheritance in Christ. Babies cannot wield the power of the Lord you have to be a grown up mature son in him. John said as many as received him to them he gave the power to become the sons of God. John 1:12 we are children of the Spirit of God we are not of the world system. We are the Ambassadors of Christ in the Earth. We are his descendants.

We are the righteous seed of God in the world today yes we are his incorruptible seed 1 Peter 1:23. This is what we are in the Lord this is not going to happen this is now. This is the reality of your status in Christ Jesus. But you have to understand that this is given to you by faith so it can only be received by faith, which you get from out of the word of God. ***Learn to speak things away from you, and learn to speak things that will come to you Mark 11:23.***

As you stay in the word and confess it out aloud daily it will grow faith in your heart. It may not seem so at times but it is working and the word will become what you say in the process of time. Always speak to your self and the Lord about who you are in him. Daily speak the word to satan and his forces and they will flee from you James 4:7. If you stay with the word night and day you will begin to see the word work for you but you must keep on speaking the word as a lifestyle. It can't be just for a few weeks or month only but this must become your life style daily. Meditate and speak the word of God day and night like the man in Psalms 1 and you will then take root in the realms of the Spirit Psalms 1:3.

This is how you will rapidly grow up in the things of God. Yes you believe but now you must say it all the time several times daily. Declare very often daily your divine status in the Christ Jesus. Remember Jesus said "You shall have whatever you say" Mark 11:23 and Numbers 14:28. <u>*As you have spoken into my ears saith the Lord so will I do unto you*</u>! The invisible spirit world always, take every word you say very serious. There is something supernatural about the tongue of every man, we have not understood it the way we should but there is a mystery regarding the tongue of man. Supernatural power of life and death is on the tongue of man. This is a spiritual law that God sets when he made man in Himself. Look how great God is yet he does nothing in this world until men speak it out of their mouths. You must remember this divine law, you must understand that satan can't turn what you say when you learn to talk like God, and you do this by speaking the promises of God every day.

Many of us even in the pulpit ministry have not grasped this yet. God waits for man to speak his word then he will manifest his power in this world. If you look at the life of every man of God they all had to say what God said in order for it to happen in this earth. Jesus operated this daily when we walked the earth.

We are sent here on purpose and destiny we are unstoppable in Christ Jesus our Lord. You have arrived because you are in the anointing and the anointing is in you always. We are sons with divine rights and status this is why we have been given the Indwelling Holy Spirit so we cry out Abba father! Abba Father! Galatians 4:5-7. This is because you are a son a descendant of the Lord God.

CHAPTER 8

MIRACLE MENTALITY MIRACLE ATTITUDE

God wants you to learn to speak His Miracle Working Language. Let the word of Christ dwell in you richly Col. 3:16. Let this Mind/Attitude/ Spirit/Faith be in you that was, in Christ Philippians 2:5. Nothing shall be impossible Matthew 17:20. It shall obey you. Luke. 17:6 there is a realm inside of us where we can receive all we need from the Lord and so finish the work we are called to do and go home to be with the Lord in glory. Keep thine heart with all diligence for out of it flows the issues/springs of life Prov 4:23.

For, as he thinks in his heart/spirit so is he. Proverbs 21:7. All things are possible to him that believeth Mk 9:23. There is a language that devils can't handle. Your whole future is decided by the words of your own mouth, you dictate your future with your tongue. Jesus said "you shall have what you say" Mark 11:23.

The mind must be taught the language of God. There is a language that sickness and disease is afraid of. The language of the living God. There is a language that poverty and every kind of distress is terrified of. There is a language that brings change to nations and communities. There is a language that sets the captive free. There is a language that brings on rain and revival and this is the language of the faith of the word of God that we need to learn to speak out daily as a lifestyle. This is how Jesus operated in his earth walk by the faith of God in him. If you ever learn to talk like God daily I tell you by the word of the Lord you will see the glory of the Lord in your life with miracles signs and wonders.

God's language is all powerful his language is omnipotent **Mark 9:23** above was spoken just before Jesus healed this boy that was in hell on earth because of Satan. The lad was dumb and deaf, plus he was prone to having fits very often which let him fell into water and fire. So you can clearly see that the Devil was out to kill him. This was dangerous stuff yes, this was an impossible situation that only God could fix. But there is a language. But there is a word Satan can't handle. Take the word and strike the enemy down give no place to hide.

Descendants of God need to learn to speak the language of the Living God. The father of the boy had come to the Church but the Church failed to help him just like the modern mix up Church today. We are full of talking skills but we lack the power to truly represent Jesus Christ. Thus the needs of the people are not been met the way God planned. Where is the miracle ability of God in the Church? Many are coming for help and we ARE SENDING THEM HOME THE SAME WAY THEY CAME TO US. This will have to stop in the name of Jesus as we take on Miracle Mentality found in the Word of God. Can you see how desperate the boy and the father were? And we could not help him with unbelief in our hearts. Unbelief is a killer of good people it is a killer of nations. It is the killer of mighty ministries.

Don't let unbelief shut the ***Blessing*** out of your life. Heb 4:1-4. This demon has stolen many of our blessings over the generations but God is now exposing how to deal with this demon of unbelief. This demon blinds one to the reality of what and who we are and get one to focus only on the natural seen things of this life. This demon loves to get us to disregard the word of God and turn only to man for help but don't let this happen to you. Make sure you spend proper time in the word and prayer so your faith life is built up in the word of faith. This is what even Jesus did all his life so when the power was needed all he did was to speak the word and it was done by the Holy Spirit. Jesus spent proper time in the word yes he was a bible reader just like you. Study Luke 4.

You remember I told you Jesus always said what he was in the word. Not what men said but what God said about him in the word was the main things Jesus spoke while he was here. This is the secret you have to learn to do the same. He even healed in line with the word. Matthew 8:16-17. In dealing with the spirit of unbelief we are dealing with wicked spirits coming from the invisible pit of hell. These spirits operate in the invisible realm. These spirits have only your destruction on their minds. They are 100% here to take you out of the war. They don't take holidays so you can't. The purpose of the Devil is to steal kill and destroy man. ***"I am come that they might have life and have it more abundantly" John 10:10.***

When we examine the text in Mark 9:23, we find that the Lord was upset with the Church because the Church was not doing its job, to cast out devils and heal the sick. The father was very disappointed because the Church had failed him so bad with the world looking on. When they talked to the Lord later he told them it was because they did not believe and they also needed to fast and pray to deal with that kind of devil. So we see prayer and fasting is vital to waging war against satanic powers in the invisible world. Many are facing the enemy unprepared but this is dangerous. So, it was a lack of focus on the **Miracle Mentality** Words of Jesus that cause the failure. It was the will of God to do it but they did not believe that they could do it so the enemy refused to go when they gave the command.

Let this mind be in you with was also in Christ Jesus Philippians 2:5. Have you ever sat and thought for a day or two of the kind of mind that was in the Son of God Jesus? He had a supernatural mindset all the time. Jesus had a miracle attitude and those who spent time with him became like him, producers of miracles. We cannot think like the world and think to please God no, we have to learn to adopt the mind of Jesus and you can only get that from the word of God by study and meditation daily. Let this mind be in you that was in Christ Jesus. With a miracle mind like Jesus we will then live a life style of miracles. With miracles we can then win much people into the kingdom of Christ. The gospel was never meant to be preached without miracles but because we have lost our miracle mentality there is not the proper flow of miracles as the Lord intended it to be in the local Church. Jesus said these signs shall follow them that believe Mark 16:15-20.

It is very clear in the word that God's plan for man has never change. Even after more than 6000 years the plan is still the same, Gen 1:28. Behold I give you power over all the power of the enemy. Luke 10:19. Man was created by the miracle working God. We were given the miracle nature of God so we could operate like him. Man is God's greatest miracle in the universe. The greatest creature that God has made is man because God made man his sons, his family. Every thing that God made was made for the benefit of man. Jesus said heaven and earth shall pass away but my words shall not pass away. This is the kind of power that is in the mouth of the descendants of God, the sons of God on earth.

If Jesus said it we can say the same thing, for it is written for us to say it as well. David said I will say of the Lord Psalms 91. Man has within him Godlikeness yes the ability of the living God was given to man so man could rule the whole earth with his voice packed with faith-filled force-filled words. Jesus said "nothing shall by any means hurt you" Luke. 10:19. Man was created a Descendant of the living God, miracle mentality was given to man to operate from the dawning of time in the Garden of Eden.

Man was given the opportunity to rule, to fix, to control, to be fruitful, in the earth all the time, in all generation. Miracle mentality was the key to this power being exhibited by the Holy Spirit in man. The time has come for you to see yourself doing the impossible with God's word in your mouth. Such as you have give, it out and you will see the power of God in demonstration daily. We have Miracle power in our mouth but we have not been using it the right way. Gen 6:11. Nothing shall be restrained from them. The body of Christ must stop talking and thinking like the world, because Satan is using our own voice to hurt us big time. We empower the devil with our negative voice/words.

You were made to live a lifestyle of Miracles signs and wonders daily Acts 2:22. This is the plan of God for the body of Christ in the earth today. This will never change because God cannot change like men do. Be like Mary she said; "be it unto me according to thy word" and Jesus was born into the earth for the benefit of all men. Get rid of your tradition and in the box thinking. Get rid of every limited way of thinking and get out of the box and prove the word of God daily in your life. Enter by faith into the realms of the power flow of the Holy Spirit.

Jesus returned in the power of the spirit after prayer in the wilderness of Judea for forty days Luke. 4. And you have the same blessing/power on you for you are a new creation in Christ you are a son of the God of heaven. The blessing of the Lord is on you all the time. Psalms 3:8. "Thy Blessing is upon thy people" Psalms 3:8. Curse not the people for they are blessed, Numbers 22:12. Man can't curse you when God has blessed you! Genesis 12:2-3. You are the descendant of God. Gen 1:26-28. Jesus said all things are possible to the man who believes the word of God and do as it says always. We are told to be doers of the word not just hearers only but doers of the word James 1:22. The impossible becomes possible with the man that does the word Matt 17:20.

You remember when Jesus said he who does the word is like the man who built his house upon the rock and not the systems of this world. Make sure on a daily basis you are doing what God told you to do in his word learn to operate just like the Lord Jesus Christ the Son of God. Miracle mentality and attitude takes time to grow, it does not come over night. But if you stay with the word and, keep it in your mouth, the word will change you and your situation will be turned around by the word in your mouth. The more resistance you get don't give up just double the dose of the word you are using.

There will be no adverse side effect as you use the word. Stay with it all the time until you know who you are in Christ and you start doing his works again in the earth John 14:12. He that believeth on me the works that I do shall he do also. Nothing shall be impossible unto you, nothing Matt 17:20. Everything that is in the natural is coming from the invisible. The invisible realm is the creative realm and it has always been so. What you see with your natural eyes is not all there is. There is much, much more than what we all see in this world.

It's a done deal with faith in your mouth.

Jesus said you shall have whatever you say Mark 11:23. Whatever God has said in his word is a done deal; it is already a reality in the realms of the supernatural. That which is to be done is already done Ecclesiastes 1:9.

God's word is God's thoughts, full of miracle power and victory therefore, as we meditate on the word and speak them daily we will develop the mentality of the God-kind of faith. Yes as we spend time in the word we will become God-inside minded. The bible says his word was with power and authority and they healed the sick and raised the dead.

That same power is in your tongue right now so you can do the same. You may not feel like it is but if God said it then it is so. There is always power in the word of God and that power is miracle power. This power is also unlimited to the ones who will believe God's word daily. It comes to us through hearing daily/consistently the word of God. Not by feelings or by sight but by hearing the word. For we walk by faith not by sight 2 Corinthians 5:7. You are the descendant of the Living God therefore you must let his Miracle Mentality grow in you. This is accomplished as you study and speak the word daily. Walk by faith. Faith cometh by hearing and hearing, by the word of God Rom 10:17. Whatever we want done in this life faith is the way to get it done. So we see that the only way to get faith is in the word of God. Faith cometh by report God's report creates faith in the hearts of men. John 6:1-2. Says

GREAT MULTITUDES FOLLOWED HIM BECAUSE OF THE MIRACLES which he did on them that was diseased. They came to hear and be healed by him.

Hear and be healed right now.

The Jesus that healed two thousand years ago is the same Jesus now. Yesterday today and forever Jesus is the same. Heb 13:8. His nature cant change his nature is his word. The basic things of God are all miraculous! We see him in Genesis 1 as the miracle worker by nature. We see him in the New Testament Church as a wonder worker by nature and this will never stop because, Jesus is alive and well and he loves people. Jesus healed people because he is Full of Compassion therefore he sent none away empty as the Church is doing now but He healed them all as the scripture declares. Every thing about the Lord is miraculous because that is His nature always, so this will never change.

The basic nature of God is <u>miracle nature</u> He does not find it hard to do any miracle, for with him nothing shall be impossible. Whatever He says becomes what He says. He word is creative force and when he made man he gave him the same power inbuilt within. He made us with the same potential to do the impossible with his word ability in our mouth. This is why he said all things are possible to him who believes Mark 9:23. Whether we are many or few it does not matter, when we have faith in God we can do what he says we can do. We can do the impossible with his word in our mouth. This is the miracle mentality that Jonathon had in his mouth and heart. He said what was in his heart and it came to pass in the natural. You must learn to talk faith in order to see the flow of God's power and glory.

There is no restraint or limit to the Lord who can save by many or by few 1 Samuel 14:6 Jon-a-thon said there is no restraint/no limit to God and we in the New Testament must say the same for God is still the Same and we are in covenant with him forever. Covenant people are indestructible people covenant people cannot be defeated. Covenant people are more than conquerors no matter what we face. Romans 8:31-32. In all these things we are more than conquerors.

Don't let satan mess with who you are in Christ. Satan has been lying to us for generations not wanting us to develop our miracle mentality in the word. Telling us that we cannot do what we are instructed to do in the word. He sends many voices through the problems of life to get our focus off the word. Even with Jesus Satan questioned his identity. Matt 4. His tactical nature don't change he is still a liar and the father of lies John 8:44. But, if God has told us something to do, he gives us the power in his word to bring it to pass in the natural world. It is not us who does the miracle but the miracle working word of God in our mouth. That word of promise must be spoken out of our mouth In order for it to be activated in our lives and circumstances. Jesus said you shall have whatever you say.

Mark 11:23. Miracle Mentality, Miracle Attitude. Let the mind of Christ be in you daily.

The mind of Christ which is the word of God is available to all believers. His mind and will develop in us as we spend time alone with him in the meditation of his word. All miracles of Jesus was as, a result of "Miracle Mentality Miracle Attitude".

The word/thoughts of God planted in man will change any adverse situation.

It will remove any kind of sickness or disease. I will take all sickness away from you Deuteronomy 7:15. It is the word in your mouth that does the work it is not by the wisdom of man but by God's wisdom in your mouth. When you are speaking God's word you are releasing spiritual forces into your life. Spiritual forces are far superior, to natural forces, because the natural forces came out of the spiritual. All things came from the invisible realms of God. John 1:1-4. The invisible realms, is always the superior realm, the power realm.

Now we can operate by faith in the invisible world using the word of God that comes from the invisible realm of God. This is why we need to learn to focus our faith to get what we need. The just shall live by faith. Hebrews 10:38 the invisible realm is 100% well organised. God's realm is perfect in the invisible world just beyond the natural realms but you need to remember the power to affect the invisible is on your tongue. Now if you learn to affect the invisible, with your voice of faith, by speaking the word daily you will then see change come to you in the natural realms. It is only a matter of time before you do because it is growing and must break forth. Now you must not be impatient it will happen as you declare it.

Remember "with God nothing shall be impossible" Matthew 17:20. You were created not to be buffeted by the world system but for reigning on Earth. You were created in the Word to crush the impossibilities of life. Your job is to VETO the works of the Devil with God's word in your mouth Luke 10:19. We are to reign as a Kings on the earth, by Jesus Christ the anointed one and His anointing Rom 5:17.

This is how God wants you to operate in this world. You as a born again new creature in Christ must learn to control your circumstances no matter how it may seem impossible. We are able to do this with God's word in our mouth. Remember the only word that will work for you personally are the ones you speak out daily. Hold onto what God said and say it all the time and your faith will grow daily. The words you speak daily will shape your tomorrow. Your future is in your tongue right now so it is up to you what you will release from your mouth. You shall have whatever you say. Mk 11:23. Your words will find you and ambush you later.

God's word spoken out of your mouth will bring on change in your daily life, it will take time but things will have to line up with the word that comes out of your mouth. Why? The same power that was in the mouth of Jesus is in our mouth. <u>Luke 21:15. Luke 10:19.</u> I give you Power over all the power of Satan. His word in your mouth is still omnipotent and you have been given power over all the power of the enemy. Now you can't see what is going on in the invisible so just trust God.

God said, "Be blessed, be fruit-full multiply Subdue and dominate Genesis 1:28. These words were the first words man ever heard. The words of the Blessing. The Blessing is the highest Authority heaven has ever given to man on earth. It is the highest power on Earth and devils and Angels must bow to it. The Blessing is far superior to the enemy because it is God himself on man. It is God in man on man and with man. This is why we need to think like the Blessing in order for it to flow like rivers of living waters.

Out of your belly shall flow rivers of living water John 7:37-38. You are the descendant of God with His blessing on you.

Where in the bible can you show anyone where God has ever given Satan power over man? Friend you will never find it in the word of God. Would you give Satan power over your children or your home? I think not. Satan is a defeated foe and must we deal with him by the faith of God in us daily. The only effective way to deal with him is with God's word in your mouth all the time. **Miracle Mentality Miracle Attitude!**

Please make sure your faith life is growing daily in the Lord by feeding your spirit and soul/mind on the written word of God daily. You do this by confessing the word. Stop your struggling and take God at his word. Agree with God's word believe it and confess it out loud. Really you aught to agree with the word of God all the time no matter what you see in the natural. You aught to train yourself to agree with what God said about you and develop the life style of agreement with God's word.

This is what the Lord did daily in spite of what he saw in the natural. This was the secret of his success on Earth. Jesus was sent to get you back on course, he said I am come that they might have life and have it more abundantly John 10:10. When you had received Christ as your Lord, the very life and nature of God was imparted to your inner man, which is the real you. You are a spirit just like God on the inside with his life, nature, being and, substance in you. You are an eternal being just like God on the inside.

We can operate in this world just as Jesus did in his earth walk. You should be producing miracles signs and wonders because you have Jesus in you right now as we talk. Christ in you the hope of Glory Col 1:27, this is what you carry in you daily. But you need to walk in the revelation understanding of who you are in him. That same Miracle MENTALITY that you carry in you, is the same power flow that was in the Lord Jesus Christ and the early Church. If you learn to talk like Jesus and think miracle thoughts like him then you will see his power flowing out of you for signs miracles and wonders. Learn to see him in you and learn to do as he say's and you will enter the realm of miracles. Your heart has been broken so many times but your time has come. Rise and act on the word and glory will hit your life.

Miracle MENTALITY means things are about to change for God have heard your prayers and seen your tears. 2 Chronicles 20:5. The new creation people in Christ are, for SIGNS, MIRACLES and you are for WONDERS. Isaiah 8:16. You are what God says you are, and you can do what God has called you to do! Bless you. The miracle mind of the Lord Jesus is available to us in the word of God.

Miracle mentality was in the heart of young Jonathon. He was facing mass enemies but that did not stop him because he was thinking in line with the covenant blessing of Abraham that was on his life as a young man of God. He was not a prophet but he took God at his word and he said there is no restraint 1 Samuel 14:6.Which meant nothing is too hard with God on my side. With this faith attitude he was able to destroy the camp of the enemy and so can you with the Blessing on your life showing your miracle mentality. Go back to the word today and get miracle mentality no matter what you face you will be able to kill it with the word of God flowing out of your mouth. **What you face is not bigger than the God you have in you right now.**

Take the blood of Jesus and strike down your enemies for He that is in you is greater than all you can see that is coming against you. Satan cannot resist you when you grow daily in miracle mentality like Jesus. You overcome Satan by the blood of, the Lamb and by the word of your testimony your testimony being what God said, about you in his word. There is no restraint to the Lord by many or by few. Jonathon was not perfect but he loved and served God even in a bad family situation. He was a blood covenant minded man of God that loved the man of God that God had called above his own father.

So you can see he was a kingdom minded man of God. Jesus said we aught to seek the kingdom first and all things would be added unto us. They fell before Jonathon and so they will have to bow to you as well, because you have already won in Christ Jesus our Lord. You have won in Christ Jesus your substitute. God has already given us the victory in Christ this is why we live by the faith of God's word. If it is by faith it is already a done deal in the realms of the spirit. Miracle mentality means that which is done is that which shall be done.

Noah had miracle mentality because there had never been a great flood before so. His generation thought he was mad to be building such a large boat on dry land. But he knew God could not lie so he kept on building for many years until the Ark was finished. The people of the world walking by sight could not understand, but we serve the God of signs and wonders. As soon as the Ark was complete God did what he said he would do many years before regardless of what the people thought. The flood came and, took them all away. Study Genesis 6. One of the main reason God had to wipe man off the earth back then, was because all the thoughts of man was completely evil all the time. The same thing is taking place again so look for God to take action.

Much wickedness is taking place in the earth today but God will destroy the earth with fire this time not a flood but with fire. The time has come to think and speak only what God has said about us just like Noah in his time.

The world may mock us and say we are mad but if we are obeying the Lord we will always come out on top all the time.

The days of Noah was evil days but, just like back then, people today have gone mad and lawless but, God took care of the matter then as he will again with the return of Jesus Christ our king. To truly become successful we have to think like how God thinks and then talk like how God talks in his word. This is how we allow the power of God to shape our future. Let this mind be in you which was in Christ Jesus our Lord Phil 2:5. Get the mind of Christ and use it daily. 1 Corinthians 2:16. The mind of Christ is a supernatural mind not a natural mind it is a mind full of the will and thoughts of the almighty God and you have it in the word.

His mind is available to us in the word all the time. When Jesus confronted Satan in the wilderness he used the mind of God which is the word of God to stop the Devil. You notice satan was trying to mess up how Jesus was thinking. If he could do that he would mess up his identity as he is doing to, many today. Many of us don't know who we really are even though God has told us over and over again in His holy word. The way to fix this is to go back to the word and internalise what God has said about us in his word. Genesis 1:28 is a good start. Be aware that you are blessed all the time and you can think the thoughts of God. Say them and get your miracle just like others around the world today. You have it in you just be conscious of it, all the time like Jesus. Train your self to know who you are in Christ in the word that is where you will find your true self. The word will show you what your rights and privileges are in the kingdom of God.

Satan can't intimidate you when you truly know who you are in the Lord Jesus. But, grow in grace and in the knowledge of our Lord Jesus Christ, 1 Peter 5. Get acquainted with your heavenly father daily spend proper time with him in the word. You have his nature in you so you will make it big time if you align yourself with his word. You are the descendant of the Most High and you have miracle mentality in you.

CHAPTER 9

WE ARE PARTAKERS OF HIS DIVINE NATURE

God hath given unto us all things that pertain, to life and to Godliness 2 Peter1 1:4 whereby are given unto us exceeding great and precious promises that by these we become partakers of the divine nature. We have the divine nature of God in us. We are immortal beings on the inside.

The nature of God in man makes man a supernatural being just like God. The only being that is called sons of God is man 1 John 3:3. We should be called the sons of God. The problems we face in this world are not normal they are coming from the dark side of the spirit world where the Devil is hiding and from there he is attacking mankind with all kinds of problems daily. So for man to make it we need a force stronger than the devil and this force is the nature of God given to us in Christ Jesus our Lord. We are the descendants of God with his nature inside of us all the time. We are born of His word sperm/seed 1Peter 1:23.

Greater is he that is in you than he that is in the world 1 John 4:4.

The righteousness nature of God is deposited within the spirit of the believer from the moment we are born again, the new birth is perfect in every way. When we received Christ it was then that we received the indestructible life nature of God. We have his life in us now as believers. We are not saved because we go to Church and do Church activities but because we have the divine nature of God in us. Being born again not of corruptible seed but of the incorruptible by the word of God which liveth and abideth forever 1 Peter, 1:23. In looking at the above scripture it is very clear that we are no longer ordinary people when we have the nature of God himself in us. Jesus is special because he made it possible for man to receive the very core of God's being substance and nature. This is what we are, this is what we have in us.

We are a very special people above all nations of the world God told Moses to tell us. Duet 7:1-8. We carry his nature in our recreated spirit. Your spirit is, you and you, are reborn/born again in Christ Jesus with his life nature in you all the time. You are one of the sons of light you are from the light world realms not the natural realms. Jesus said ye are the light of the world. Remember that you are a spirit with a soul living in a flesh body. 2 Corinthians, 4:6-8 but we have this treasure in earthen vessels. Vessels meaning our body!

Now it is very vital that you see in the spirit that you are the partaker of the very life nature of God almighty through Jesus Christ the son of God. We are the partakers of the very resurrection life nature that was in Christ Jesus our Lord. We are descendants of the Most High God with his nature in us Col. 3:4 declares that Christ is our life and we are to set our minds/affection on things above & not on things on the earth. God wants us to focus on who, and what he is in us, and who we are in Christ Jesus. We are to be growing in the knowledge of who we are in the master Jesus because it is as we do this we will be able to fully represent him on the earth. Acts 1:8 ye shall be witnesses unto me in all the earth.

Because of a lack of knowledge of who we are in Christ many are falling down at this time. My people are destroyed for lack of knowledge. Not power but knowledge. This is a tragic thing going on in the body of Christ today. We have laid aside the word of God for the traditions of this wicked generation that know no boundaries in wickedness.

To partake of a thing is to be one with the thing you, are partaking off. This is how it is in the spirit, as we partake of the word and fellowship the Holy Spirit we become one with him by blood covenant rights. The perfect John chapter 15 explains it so greatly. Jesus is the vine and we are the branches of the supernatural Vine life of God himself.

Branches are always one with the vine life nature of any tree. We are the branches of God's nature his power his ability his success his love and so on and on it goes on unlimited. Behold I give you power over all the power of the enemy Luke 10:19 Sounds like Gen. 1:26 to me. Why did he say behold? It is because you can only see this by faith in your heart. You are the descendant of the living God you are a partaker of his supernatural life nature. You are his family on earth. You are one with him in your spirit. That which is born of the spirit is spirit. John 3:1-6. He that is joined unto the Lord is one spirit, so it is no longer us but him within us now. 1 Corinthians 6:17.

The Vine and the Branches are one

Jesus explains who we are in the 15th chapter of John. "He said I am the vine ye are the branches. Now just as the vine and the branches need each other to fulfil purpose so it is that the body of Christ need Jesus who is the vine to which the branches belong. In him we are complete Colossians 2:10 "Without him we can do nothing" John 15. We cannot do anything without being in the vine Life nature of Jesus Christ.

Jesus was trying to show us how close we are to him when he talked about the vine and the branches. Now all that is in the vine flows at all times to the branches which is what we are in Christ. The believer is a branch of Jesus Christ himself who is the son of the living God. Now if we are branches of Christ who is really God himself then we are Descendants of the living God with his life and divine nature inside each of us who received Christ. This is what Peter is talking about when he said we are partakers of the divine nature of God himself.

This is real, this is what we really are, in the Lord but many, in the body are not taking advantage of our birth rights in Christ. The divine royal nature of the living God is hidden deep within the believer.

Something supernatural happened when we received him as Saviour and Lord of our lives. We became sons of God when we accepted Jesus Christ into our hearts. We share in his divine nature which is 100% supernatural all the time. We can take on any task given to us by God or Man because of the nature of God in us all the time. The nature of God in man changes a man yes it brings on spiritual refinement. This is where we connect back to God yes this is what religion cannot give you. With the impartation of divine nature in us comes all that God really is in us. Understand that nothing is too hard for divine nature, nothing at all.

Jesus said all things are possible unto him that believeth. Mark 9:23. As thou hast believed so be it done unto you. Matthews 8:13.

So what is the nature of God? It is what God is it, is eternal life the nature of the great father God. It is the life that Adam had before he fell in the Garden of Eden. It is the very same life that was in Jesus in his earth walk 2000 years ago. This life nature was what was in Jesus all the time. It is the miracle working life nature of God in man capable of doing the impossible. This is what you have in you all the time as a believer in Christ Jesus our Lord.

The word declares that "**The word of the Lord is very pure**" and this is what you are made of as a believer. Never let this go from your heart. Psalms 119:163.

It is the highest blessing man can get from the Lord. Heaven has nothing better than the life nature of the creator to offer to man. In him was life and the life was the light of men John 1. Man cannot be enlightened without the Son of God Jesus Christ. Jesus came into the world to give us back the light of God that we lost in Eden. The nature of God is perfect and timeless it cannot get old as things, in the natural world does. God loves man so much that he has given back to man the very nature of himself in the new birth. This is why he says we are partakers of divine nature 2 Peter 1:1-4. What is the nature of God? The nature of God is compassion. The word says he is full of compassion.

Really with His nature in you, you are full of compassion as well. Compassion is always seeking how to help others. You are here to solve problems. This is the nature of the Spirit of compassion which is the nature of the living God. The believer is a partaker of all this in his spirit. Compassion is your father so go show compassion. Creation is the result of compassion. Your father is compassion. Jesus was moved by compassion. Compassion created the world.

You understand from what we have been talking about that man is basically a spirit being just like God capable of operating on the same level of faith like God. This is why we needed back the nature of God that was lost in the fall of man in the days of the first Adam in Eden. Jesus came as the son of man the representative of man the second Adam and gave is back the nature of God in the new birth. In the new birth that is a product of God's word the nature is back in man so we can now relate to God as Adam did before he fell. God is back in man on the Earth again in the nature he has given us in Christ. We are the descendants of God yes and we have his nature in us right now. We are the off springs of the living God.

The body of Christ is not about religion but it is about the nature of God almighty in man. Given to us is the very ability of God to strike the enemy Matthew 18:18-20. We have his nature back. We in these end times have this unlimited nature ability of God in us. The more we get into the word and study these things is the more we will tap the unlimited might of the living God so we can help our generation.

Within the nature of God is all we need for this life and the life to come in the next world. There is nothing greater in heaven than what the believer already have within. It was compassion the nature of God that saved us from our sins and wrote our names in heaven. Been a sinner is the worst thing that one could be and this is what we were but his compassion nature stepped in and rescued us from the pit of hell. We have his nature in us as the **Descendants of God** yes we carry his nature glory in us now. His nature in us in this wicked world comes with a mission to rescue others into his kingdom so we take his nature which is love nature, and invade this world with it.

The greatest force in this world is the love-force nature of God in man. When this nature of God gets into a man it changes him from within and gives him new life in the spirit. It is called a new creation by Paul in 2 Corinthians 5:17. We are the Descendants of the living God with his nature being and substance of faith in us. We are his rightness people in a messed up old world. The world is falling apart but we are not, for his nature sustains us all the time from within. The greatest life force in this world is His nature and this is what we have now in the new birth.

You want to see some Proof? Being born again, not of corruptible seed, but of the incorruptible, by the word of God, which liveth and abideth for ever, 1 Peter 1:23.

"You are Success-full" "You are fruit-full" Genesis 1:28.

We partake of his Success-full nature his nature is the winning-full nature in us. The winning–full nature of the living God is in us all the time to put us over in life. We don't have to be victims no more we can change that now with his nature in us. I am come that they might have life that that more abundantly. That life is what God is. It is called eternal life in the word of God and this is what we have in us of God. If we are partakers of the nature of God as his sons then we are the forever family of God himself. You notice Jesus said that I go to prepare a place for you in my fathers house John 14:1-2. We can live in his house because we are his sons and daughters with his nature imparted to all of us who truly believe. And because ye are sons God hath sent forth the spirit of His son in our hearts crying Abba father. Galatians 4:5-6.

The success-full nature of God is given to you. So success is no problem for you. All you have to do is take his word and change how you see yourself daily. You are success waiting to explode yes it is in you right now You have in you the success-full Spirit of God in you all the time 24 hours per day he is in you to help you not to push you down but to help you into purpose and your End times destiny. Mindset is now our major problem so deal with it with the word of God and remember his nature is in his word. Let this mind be in you which was also in Christ Jesus the Lord!

How do we deal with the wrong mindset? We begin to confess what God say out of our mouth all the time until the word give us a new divine miracle mindset. To have the mindset of God is, to be able to do the impossible. Nothing shall be impossible unto you. Matthew 17:20. But you will have to take the time to labour in the word day and night until faith comes. If you put his word in your mouth you are putting his nature in you. His nature is miracle nature his nature in omnipotence His nature in you will force all that is anti-covenant in your life to line up with the word of his nature in your mouth. He said, "**Whatever he doeth shall prosper**" Psalms 1. YOU ARE THE PERSON HE IS TALKING ABOUT IN THIS PSALMS?

With His nature in us, no weapon formed against us shall prosper. So we rise to the top and excel/abound because of his success-full nature in us. His nature to put us over and make us winners in this world is within. You have his nature in you and you are his Descendant. You can take it by force because you have nature force in you to put you over all the time in this world. He planned no defeat for you. 1 John 4:4 ye are of God little children and have overcome them because greater is that Iain you than he that is in the world.

God expects us to win all the time because Jesus has already won and we are now to live our lives on Earth by the faith of Jesus Christ in us. You carry His nature in you so be bold and daring on his word. You are not of this world system you are of God; you are an ambassador of Christ. You are what the word of God say's you are regardless of feelings!

Caleb was a very successful man because he trusted God's Success-full words regardless of what he saw in the natural for 40 years. Even when he was an old man at 85 he was still killing giants and taking mountains with "success" full words in his mouth Numbers 13 & 14 study. I don't know what you face today, but you already have in you what it takes to whip the situation that seems impossible. You have his nature in you right now. You can do the impossible with the power of God on your tongue. The same God that was with Caleb is the same God that is with you right now. You are definitely the **descendant** of the highest God. Put the word of God your tongue all the time, and you will see heaven work in your life.

"**Obey my voice and I will be your God**" Jeremiah 7:23. The Lord showed me something that I will now show you now. **Take off the 'o' and the 'y'** and you will have **Be**. So God is saying "<u>**Be my voice and I will be your God**</u>". The voice of God is the word of God so be his voice in the earth by speaking his word out daily. All of God's word is success-full waiting on us to claim them then we will get the manifestation. The nature of God in the word cannot fail, so stand on the word in your heart no matter what is going on around you. As you hold the word in your heart begin to say them aloud daily to your self, then to others and you will see the Glory of God flow out of you to hurting people in the community. You are blessing-full so you are equipped with divine power.

We are a new race, of spirit beings like God. All this is on the inside of us now. Understand that you are a spirit in the likeness of the great God of Heaven. Your father is the great father of our Lord Jesus Christ the son of the Living God. This is why you are blessing full at the expense of Jesus Christ. Everything that is good is given to you by Jesus Christ.

This is why you had to be designed in a way so that you can carry the nature of the living God. Your spirit is connected to God and his power nature in you. To stir up this power in you all you need to do is pray often and speak the word all the time into your circumstances. (Openly decree, declare & confess the word of God daily) This is how the nature of God in you will rise up. Faith comes out of your heart through your mouth in word form. These words determine how your life will turn out on earth and also where you will end up forever in the spirit world. Now understand that, we are all moving forward to wards the spirit world, where we came from. We can't stay here when our time is up we will have to go to him who sent us into the world to make it a better place. Oh yes you were sent here to make the world a better place. Please check your life now to see if you are making this world a better place with divine power.

The nature of God is a spiritual nature not a natural nature. The nature of God in us is wealth-full there is no lack in God and he has never put lack in man or on man. You are a blessing-full being. You are rich-full being. You are a Joy-full being as quoted in Psalms "Thy Blessing is upon thy People". There it is. It is very clear that the nature of God is in man in the new birth. There is no birth defects in the new birth, the new birth is perfect in us. The blessing nature is the endowment to make us able to do the things God wants us to do, while we are here on the earth today. Do not waist your life and time on the earth but rise up with the nature of God and, be an asset to your generation. With his nature in you, you can do what the Lord wants you to do in this world. No one can stop you all the days of your life but you! Discipline yourself to believe in who you are. You are what the Lord says you are in his word, and remember God cannot lie.

You are blessed/endowed/equipped with his nature/power in you all the time, 2 Peter 1:1-4. You carry everything he says you have. Blessed be the God and father of our Lord Jesus who hath blessed us with all spiritual blessings in heavenly places in Christ, Ephesians 1:3.

Understand that in Christ God has held nothing back from you but has given you all things in Christ Jesus Eph 1:3. This is for this world and the next, you can enjoy your inheritance now. It is available to you by faith in the promises of the Living God. His blessing life nature is in you on you and with you forever. Gen 1:28. *"And God blessed them and said be fruit-full multiply replenish the earth."* You notice He did not say replenish the Garden but the earth. Look at the vastness of this world how! Can you now see your potential in Christ? This is what he means when he says "all things are possible to him that believeth Mark 9:23". His nature in you makes you a supernatural being that is capable of representing Jesus Christ to the whole dying world!

There is no way we can win this world for Jesus until we fully embrace the nature of Jesus Christ within us because it will take miracles signs and wonders to win this world back to Christ. People today are so far gone in sin only the nature power of the one can reach them in the darkness of sin. The enemy have them in a dark place hiding them from the light of the Gospel but we can reach them with the love nature of Jesus Christ in us today. If we truly walk in the nature of the love of Christ Jesus we will be able to take this world for Jesus, because, the greatest force in this world is still the love of God in Christ Jesus our Lord. There is nothing stronger than the Love of God. Even death, have to bow to the love of God in Christ Jesus our Lord and master.

The greatest witness we can produce to the world of the resurrection of Christ is when the body of Christ learn to walk and live daily in the love of God. We need more love in this wicked world that we see here. That love is within the hearts of the believer, but we have not let it out the way we should, but God is in the process of putting this right. So we will see the greatest revival among the nations that the world has ever seen, from the days of Paul. I truly believe this with all my heart. The greatest witness is LOVE, LOVE and LOVE! John 3:16.

Ye shall be witness unto me unto the uttermost part of the Earth he said Acts 1:8.

CHAPTER 10

DON'T SELL OUT YOUR BIRTHRIGHT INHERITANCE

And Jacob said to Esau, Sell me this day thy birthright and Esau said Behold I am at the point of death and what profit shall this birthright do me. And he sold his birthright unto Jacob, thus Esau despised his birthright as shown in Genesis 25:31-34.

The devil hates you because of your birthright your inheritance is in Christ Jesus which is over him. Now the Lord wants, me to talk about an area of the body of Christ that most of us don't want to hear about. Isaac had two sons Esau and Jacob. From the word of the Lord we clearly can see that they were two different kinds of people. Esau was a man that had no time for the things of the Spirit yet he was "the first born" of Isaac. Isaac was a man of prayer and a man of meditating the word. Isaac was a blood covenant minded man of God. He was one that loved the God of Abraham his father. He was a man who lived by the word of the living God. However, his firstborn son. Esau did not appreciate the covenant of the Lord the way he should.

Things were not right in the home in terms of what would happen with the two sons he had. The older son who in the natural should get the blessing by birth right law had no respect for it. Isaac overlooked this and was still prepared to bless Esau but God would not have it. You see the blessing are for those of us that will put the covenant first in our daily lives. Esau was a problem son with no value for the truth or the word, he was not a faith man; he simply lived by what he saw and felt.

All the time and training that Isaac had invested into Esau to take over the family and walk in the blood covenant meant nothing to this young man. He was only interested in the things of this world. For we walk by faith not by sight 2 Corinthians 5:7. In short he was a man of the flesh. He was walking by sight not faith. God needed a man that would walk by faith with him a man that would copy Abraham. But Esau had other things on his mind not the word of the Lord He was a womaniser and a man pleaser.

We all have to learn to put the things of the kingdom of God first in our lives if we want the blessing of the Lord to work in our lives. Esau put the world system that God hates as his number one priority, a system that is hostile to the kingdom word of the living God. This will not happen to you in the name of the Lord Jesus." That is a dangerous place to be, so do not go there". *Jesus said; seek first the kingdom of God and his righteousness and all things shall be added unto you.*

Esau loved his father but he did not know how to walk by faith like his father. He therefore did not obey the word in this area of covenant keeping. This is very sad as he was, the grand son of the great man of faith Abraham. He had all the time to learn from Isaac his father. But other things of the world system were on his mind. He was a man of the flesh not a man of the spirit. In these last days many of you are looking at your children and you are wondering what has happened.

The enemy has come in and stolen the minds and hearts of the children. With many parents there is no connection with their own children any more. This is the work of the devil and it will have to be shut down by the body of Christ in the name of Jesus. Don't give up on your children but go to war in the spirit for their souls. It is so sad when we see children grow up in a home of love and faith and then they turn completely over to the side of the enemy Satan. Don't sell out your inheritance. The Devil doesn't want our children to take up the faith legacy that we have received from our fathers in the spirit.

What he wants is for young people to live the way the world does and abandon the way of faith in God's word. God is about to change this, His people will no longer leave their children behind to go to hell. Jacob said "sell me your birthright." The enemy hates the birthright blessing and wants to take it away from us as he did with Adam in the Garden. Don't sell out on the Lord. Esau had it all by birth position as firstborn, but had no insight into that which he truly was.

Is it not strange how Esau could not see what he had but Jacob could see the unlimited value of the birth right blessing that was on Esau? Many times in my life it took someone else to show me what I was carrying because I did not know it. The time has come to find out what God has deposited in us for the benefit of this people in the earth. "But we have this treasure in earthen vessels" 2 Corinthians 4:7. When will the body of Christ really wake up to the reality of who we really are in the Lord Jesus Christ? The time has come to discover what we are, and what we have in the beloved. The key is revelation knowledge of the invisible things of the Spirit of the living God. We can only know what is ours by taking heed to what the Holy Spirit have to say to us in the word of God. Even Jesus found himself in the word and so will you if you take the proper time to search out the word of the living God daily.

It will take us time but a careful constant prayerful study of the word of God will always produce the results promised in the word of faith. Jesus said search the scriptures for in them ye shall find eternal life. Jesus also said that the words he speaks are words of life John 6:63. This life in the word, it is the birthright inheritance of the descendants of the living God. There can be no true success with God without revelation knowledge of his words in our hearts.

The church is much like Esau today, not respecting the finer things of the Spirit. Which is revelation knowledge; Jesus operated by revelation knowledge at all times in his earth walk with the father. Revelation knowledge is of God, knowing what God knows, and have revealed to us in his word by his Spirit. We must learn to live by revelation knowledge and not the things we see around us daily. It takes time to receive revelation knowledge download from the Lord.

This is why Psalms 1 declare that we are to meditate on the law of the Lord day and night. This is the key to breakthrough and success on the earth. This is why like Jacob, the most unusual people just come over night and take the blessings of the Lord and many in the church for years are going without as they will not obey the word of the Lord. We cannot be blessed until we obey the Lord our God. We will not really do as the Lord says until we have revelation faith in him and His holy word. He said "obey my voice and I will be your God Jeremiah 7:23".

Esau had the rights and the blessing position but did not value it the way he should. He wanted to live the way he wanted, and he did not have the covenant at heart as Jacob did. Jacob was a crook but he respected the covenant of blood. You have problems in your life but God knows that you love Him as did Jacob the con man before God changed him in Israel.

Now there was a prophetic word that the elder would serve the younger and it looked impossible that this would ever happen but; as you know by this God cannot lie and no matter how it seems in the natural the word will still come to pass as the Lord have said to us.

Jesus said the word cannot be broken and so do I John 10:35 study. Esau was a towering might of flesh and Isaac would never agree in the natural to give the blessing to Jacob but God said the elder shall serve the younger he said many years before. When God speaks it is already done. Now God did not take the blessing away from Esau. He talked himself out of his own blessing. This divine law that we shall have what we say is an eternal spiritual law. It is not a new law of God. The prophets functioned using this great law of God they knew that what they said would come to pass in the process of time. Esau knew this law that is why after what he did with Jacob over the meal he despised his birthright. Get use to the law of faith, saying before seeing.

In those days the first born were the ones with the blessing of the father; but God is no respecter of persons He is a respecter of faith in the heart of men. Esau said what good is this birthright to me and when he said that the Lord heard him in heaven. We shall have what we say Mark 11:23.

You see he did not have the love for God that Jacob had in his heart and God knew it. Understand that man is always looking at the outward appearance but God always looks into the hearts of men 1 Samuel 16. So we can fool people but not God. What ever is in the heart in abundance must come out of the mouth of man. This is how we create things in this world by speaking out of our mouth what we already have in abundance in our hearts. Matt 12:34-35. Of the abundance of the heart the mouth speaketh. Therefore if we don't like what we are seeing in our lives, we need to simply change what we are saying and say only what God says about us in His word.

How much value do you place on God's investment into your life? Are you walking by faith with God or do you put the things of the world before the Lord your God. Demas the friend left Paul and went back into the world because he loved the world more than how he Loved Jesus. Please don't let that happen to you and loose your one soul. The enemy is terrified of people who are sold out for the Lord Jesus. Jacob love the lord though he was not right with God he loved God and his covenant. He respected the God of Abraham and Isaac.

Don't let satan get you to compromise with his world system as how Jezebel got Ahab to compromise with her, and so lost all. Jezebel hated the word of the Lord in the mouth of the prophets that's why she killed most of the prophets and then she tried her best to kill Elijah but she could not. The enemy wants to kill what God has put inside of you by getting you to compromise with the way of the world but don't let him get away with it. You have the birthright inheritance in you but you have to take your mouth and put it to work for you not against you. It is not up to the Lord it is up to you because you shall have what you say as a descendant of the living God.

You have the right to get your needs met by the power of the Lord. You are a son of the living God so all your needs are met already but you have to learn to believe in what you are and what you have. Know that God lives in you all the time and you will grow very fast in the things of the Spirit. You are God's inheritance on the earth. This puts you into God's supernatural class of beings on the earth today. This is why he has given you power over all the power of the enemy, Luke 10:19.

Psalms 46, God is our refuge and strength a very present help in trouble. Never give in to the wiles of the devil because God made you a success in Christ. Yes in Christ Jesus we win all the time. You are the one with the blessing of the Lord on you so act like it tell the fear to get out of your life now. You are an over comer in the Lord Jesus so plea the blood of Jesus on the devil and sound out the word of your testimony against hell it self. Don't ever back down from what God told, you in his word, having done all just stand on the word of the living God. Resist the devil and he will flee from you.

Rebuke the devil out of your life and house. Esau was a man with no go, yet he wanted the blessing. The blessing will only work with those that will obey God at all times no matter what the case may be.

Jesus died to give you your inheritance so don't talk your self out of it like Eve in the Garden of Eden, Genesis 3. Stand your ground and say, who you are, and learn to depend on your inheritance in Christ Jesus. Stand fast in the liberty of Christ Jesus. Your time to excel has come Just like Jacob even though you may be in a fix right now and things are going so bad don't give up on your inheritance in the Lord Jesus Christ.

Esau opened his mouth and sold out on God and God had no choice but, to hearken to his voice even though later he wanted the blessing, it was too late another had taken the blessing and you cannot reverse the blessing once it has been spoken. *Curse not the people for they are blessed* Numbers 22:12. You shall have what you say and this law can't be changed not even by the Lord Mark 11:23. It is the Law that God respects all the time and it cannot fail us when we learn to tap into it by the faith of God in us. We do this by speaking Gods word to our problems.

The bible says "**cursed is the man that trust in man**" and makes flesh his arm he will not see when good cometh Jer 17. Have you ever notice how some people only see the evil and never the good? These are the kind of people the word is talking about so get away from them. Don't sell your inheritance you are **the descendant of the living God.** You are what God says you are and you have what God says you have. *As he is so are you.*

Esau said he was at the point of death Genesis, 25:32. But that was a lie from the pit of hell. He was not at the point of death plus do you think that a man like Jacob would really let his twin brother die for lack of food? I think not. But so often when we are against the wall in our lives we turn to the arms of the flesh in stead of our blood covenant God for help. When will we really recognise that we are God's covenant people that are under his divine protection all the time? And no weapon, which is formed against us, shall prosper in the name of Jesus.

As believers we should not let what we see become our main focus as Esau did in his day. We can see later how with bitter tears he tried to get the blessing back but it was too late and he found no place of repentance. His father wanted to help him but the blessing on Jacob could not be reversed. Curse not the people for they are blessed Numbers 22:12.

The blessing is what God does but satan is the one that brings on the curse however in Christ you are blessed for fever with the eternal inheritance. Heb 9 explains that Jesus obtained the eternal inheritance for us when he rose from the dead and we are with him. How sad it is to be the first born son and then lose it all because of doubt and unbelief.

Scripture declares take heed therefore brethren lest there be in any of you an evil heart of unbelief Hebrew 4.

We give room to unbelief when we talk and behave like the world and the devil. We are told to behave ourselves in the house of the living God.

Don't sell out your inheritance don't give in to the enemy of righteousness because we are the righteousness of God in Christ on the earth today. You are needed here; the world needs you and what you have on the inside. The very son of God Jesus is living in you yes the Lord is the portion of your inheritance. In Christ you have obtained an inheritance forever, Ephesians 1.

Now Esau lost out because he did not spend the time to find out about the rights that he had, he gave it up for a pot of meat. He did not value/respect his spiritual heritage. What you respect will respect you. Jacob was a thief but he loved the covenant and longed to get the first born blessing and God gave it to him because it was his dream. He went about it the wrong way but his heart was in the right place so God blessed him. Remember when God blesses it means to equip or ordain or setup or approve. When God approve you no man can put you down because, all heaven is behind you with all might. Jacob was in a mess but the blessing took care of that later on, and it also changed his life style and his heart. He was no longer after wealth but he was after God with all his heart. The Lord became his blood covenant brother.

We need to learn to put the things of God first, then we will see how God will bless us as we put the kingdom of God first. The blessing will take care of you as no other can in your life on earth. *In all your ways acknowledge him and he will direct your path Proverbs 3:1-6. Trust in the Lord with all thine heart.*

Remember your heart is your spirit that is born again in Christ Jesus. When Jacob went before Isaac and was felt by his father how, sad it was to see how bad it is to rely on the flesh. The flesh is extremely deceptive and will lie to us but God's word, will and plan cannot lie to us. The word says it is impossible for God to lie. Did you know that Jesus is actually the real truth? He said; *I am the way the truth and the life. John 14:6.*

The bible declares that, *there is no lie in the truth.* Remember that the testimony of God is sure. Jesus said *we shall know the truth and the truth shall make us free.* Jacob lied to his father to get what he wanted instead of trusting God to give the blessing to him. It took him many years to learn to walk by faith the way that he should. Jacob should have never tried to help the Lord do his part in fulfilling the covenant. That is what Sarah did and Ishmael was born of the flesh and not the promise. The family of Abraham is in much pain today because of what Sarah and Abraham did way back then. Don't try to help God it will not work.

There is no lie of the truth of God's word, it will take time but God will always do what he said he will do in his promise. This has always been so with God. This is how he is. He works by his word when he can find some one to believe him no matter what they see in this world. It is called faith in God. We are meant to live out our lives on earth by having faith in the promises of the Living God. This should become our primary way of functioning.

There is no lie of the truth and the truth is Jesus 1 John 2:21. This is who you have in you. You have Christ in you the hope of glory, Colossians 1:27. As we feed on the word daily we will become more and more like Jesus. Jacob fed on the covenant and he became a change man over the years. You are the descendant of God. You are in a blood covenant with the creator God of the whole universe. The more the enemy try to crush you is the more the anointing in your life will flow out of you. You cannot get oil out of the olive until you press the olive and so it is with you as a descendant of the living God .The more the devil press in on you is the more the power of the Lord will flow out of you and heal others. No matter what the devil tries to do to you it will back fire on him in the name of the Lord Jesus Christ.

Don't sell out on the Lord stand in the liberty that you have in Christ Jesus so that you will fulfil your destiny. You are the descendant of the living God yes you are the descendant of the blessing of the Lord. All that Jesus is in you right now. We have the new birth and it is an instant experience in ones life. Rom 10:9-10. Esau sold his birthright with words and this is how many are selling their birth today by speaking the fear words of the devil and not the faith words of the living God. You need to understand that fear-filled words connect you to Satan but faith filled words connects you to the Lord. We operate in the kingdom with our words. We use words to build up and we use them to break down.

This has always been so, it always work because it is the major law in the realm of the invisible world of God Almighty. We are in a war of words in this world. Jacob stole the birthright with words just as how Satan conned eve with words many years ago in the Garden. We need to get a clear understanding of how powerful words are in the lips of man. This is why we need to speak the words of life only, just as Jesus did in his earth walk. Death and life is in the power of our tongue.

Jacob the man who became a prince of God.

Yes, the life of Jacob is some thing to thrill the heart. First we see him stealing from his own brother then running from his brother in fear for his life. But we also see that God was still with Jacob in all his ways because God had a great plan for the life of Jacob. There are times we need to be alone with God to hear clearly what he has to say about us. Most of these times our lives may not be right with Him but if we take time out to be with Him, He will be with us and blessed us.

This is what happened to Jacob at Bethel. While he was there, "alone", in the presence of God without even, knowing it. God in his covenant mercy began to talk to Jacob. Jacob did not know he had the ears to hear from God he did not know that he was cut out to be a king Prophet but he was, as far as God was concerned.

He got a shock as the Lord started to tell him who he was and how great a destiny was ahead of him. This event, change the life of Jacob completely. It turned him into another man that wanted full fellowship with God a man walking now with God almighty. The bad things he was doing in the past caught up with him but God took care of him so he would suffer no lost. You see in the blessing we shall suffer no loss at all. The blessing covers the bad things we have done in our past with the blood.

The blessing inheritance is our divine birthright and we should never sell out on God. Jacob from the event at bethel stayed loyal to the Lord and the Lord took care of him all his life.

In Christ as sons of God we have a birth right and, an inheritance in the Lord Jesus Christ. This inheritance is incorruptible and it is laid up for us by God our father. Satan don't want you to find out about your divine birthright he wants you to be ignorant of it so, he can take advantage of you, as he is doing to many today in the body of Christ. Paul said when he was an old man "that I may know him and the power of his resurrection "and this should be our prayer as well daily Philippians 3:13-14. <u>We can only know God in his word there is no other way.</u>

Don't sell out on God as the people did in the days of Moses Numbers 14. For forty years they could not go into the promise land because of their own mouth. **Your mouth can stop you if you don't talk like God. Your future will follow your mouth** so watch your mouth all the time. No one in the promise land could stop them but their own mouth stopped them for forty years. The people as one said; *we are not able to take the land* and God had to do as they said *Numbers 14:28. "As you have spoken in my ears saith the Lord so will I do unto you"*.

That event is a lesson for all of us today in the body of Christ, and we better learn from it. The Land is ours but we have to go and take it by force, with faith-filled force-filled words Like Caleb and Joshua. May be the land you want is healing. *As thou hast believed so be it done unto thee Matt8:13*

Put the word in your mouth and, take your birthright blessing in the name of Jesus Christ the Son of the living God. You are as rich as the promises of God in your mouth. Gods word is God himself in you so don't you ever back off from what God say is yours. Your healing success and` victory is in your mouth; yes God has already given it to you in Christ Jesus our Lord. 1 Corinthians 15:54-57 Plus remember Jesus said you shall have whatever you say and when you pray you must believe you receive and you shall have them, Mark 11:23-24. It shall obey you, as emphasized in Luke 17:6 by Jesus.

You have in Christ Jesus a divine birthright to all the things God gave to you in Christ before the world began. Do you understand what it really means to be created in Christ Jesus? This is you birthright inheritance. This is an **eternal inheritance** as Paul said in Hebrews 9. Every believer is a god walking the earth today. Jesus said ye are gods, John 10:34-35. We are not God but we are gods as the sons of God having the same rights to wield the power of God, just like Jesus in his earth walk 2000 years ago.

Jesus came into the world to redeem us from the hands of Satan and to show us how to operate in the things of the Spirit of God that are freely given to us, by the blood of Jesus Christ the son of the Living God. By birth you are in the family of God and it is time to fully accept by faith the full implications of the reality of your victory in the word of God. Remember what I have been showing you that God cannot lie. Numbers 23:19 He is not a man that he should tell a lie. Jesus came with a body but he was still God almighty on the inside. He could not lie.

Many of us are like Jacob with a lot of faults in our daily life on earth, but understand that we are still chosen by God to be a part of his son. Yes you are in the divine family of the living God. *You are his descendant today.*

We have been chosen by God before the foundation of the world to be connected to his son Jesus Christ. We are connected we are accepted in the beloved Ephesians 1. The believer is a stranger on the earth waging war in enemy territory against the devil and his cohorts. We are the people that God talks about in Psalms 1 yes we are planted by the Holy Spirit by the rivers of living water and we shall never see when drought comes, because we are drawing from the divine river of, the Living God that can't run dry. Our source is totally unlimited. Whatever we do we will prosper in the name of Jesus Christ because, of the blessing inheritance on our lives, Psalms 1. Study it well. This Psalms is talking about you who obey the word of the Lord.

I use to say we are ordinary people but now I cannot say that any longer because we are not ordinary people from the moment we were born again in Christ, we passed out of the normal into the realms of the supernatural God. We are born of the word of God himself therefore we are the sons of God by birthright inheritance and this is why God says we are heirs of God and Joint heirs with Christ. Romans 8:16-17.

Most of us in the body of Christ have not accepted this remarkable thing that God has done for us in Christ. Yes, many are still trapped by their religion and tradition. But no matter what the world system say, we are still what God says we are. The new birth is your blessing from the Lord God. It is the greatest thing that has ever happened to man after the fall of Adam in the Garden of Eden. This is what makes you a part of God Himself because he has given you all of himself in his word.

The new birth makes you an ambassador of the kingdom of almighty God himself, 2 Corinthians 5:17-21. You are joined unto the Lord God by blood covenant, this covenant is an everlasting covenant Hebrews 12. There is no way blood covenant can be broken, this is why Jesus said; the scripture cannot be broken John 10:35. "My covenant, will I not break." Time can't affect the word of God because time is temporary but the word is eternal and will always be eternal. Remember that it was the word that made time itself so how can time be greater than what made it? **Time is not creative but the word is creative.**

Jacob had to learn over the years to let God do things for him and, not walk in the flesh yes he learnt to walk by faith Just, like his dad and Abraham did before him.

He learnt to spend time with God alone on the hills of Padanaran. Those days were very lonely some times but God was grooming Jacob for greatness. He did not understand that one day he would be in Egypt's blessing the Pharaoh of Egypt.

God has a good plan for your life on earth, so don't sell out on him like Esau. Learn to walk by faith in his word and he will take care of you. Remember he is a faith God who will at all times respond to your faith in his word to you, he is not trying to hurt you but to help you into your divine purpose and destiny. This he planned for you many years ago before you were sent to the earth Ephesians 2:10. You are his workmanship in Christ.

Don't listen to people who condemn you because of the things you face in your life, just keep your eyes on the Lord and what he did for Jacob he will do for you. It may be a sickness you face or a bad marriage or unemployment or some other thing that is trying to rule over you. But don't give up your faith. Go back to the word of the Lord and he will show you what you must do in order to get your miracle from him. There is no case too hard for the Lord to help you, so refuse to let your blessing go like Jacob who said *"I will not let you go until you bless me"* Genesis 31.

There are times in our lives when we will have to roll up our sleeves and fight for what belongs to us just, as Jacob did. Gen 31. *Don't let Satan get any place in your life cast him out.*

The man fought with an angel. Friend we have never seen this before, a man fought an angel and won with his faith. Whatever you know God has given you in his word, there are times you have to go to war, to get them manifest because the enemy will always, come to try to block what is ours in the Lord. Paul said *fight the good fight of faith. Give no place to the devil* resist him and he will flee from you. To stand your ground against the devil you have to use the word of the Living God. God's word in your mouth is a done deal. Nothing in this world can stop the word of God in your mouth when you speak it in faith.

Faith filled words dominates the Law of sin and death Romans 8:1 study. Faith-filled words will dominates any kind of, sickness or circumstances that you face in your life. The language of God is still the greatest force in this world. God's language is the words of faith. It took the walls of Jericho down flat so our troops could walk on flat ground into Jericho. You have the birth right to miracles signs and wonders with the blessing inheritance of the Lord on your life.

All that is good comes from the blessing inheritance on your life. We don't have to be perfect for God to bless us; it is our inheritance in Christ Jesus. So receive the blessings, take it by faith and his wonderful blood that redeems us from all evil. Our birthright comes to us by the rights of our redemption in Christ. Ephesians 1:7 states *"In whom we have redemption* through his blood". He is talking to you and about you. So all we have in Jesus came to us by his precious blood. Those of us that are wise will learn to place unlimited value in the ability of the blood of Jesus. Without his blood there could be no redemption so we thank God for the blood.

Your blessing comes in two forms invisible then visible believe you receive them in your spirit man then you shall have them in your natural. Mark 11:24 when you study the life of Jacob you will see how he had to fight the good fight of faith to keep the blessing on him. Satan tried to break him in every way he could but Jacob would not give in. There was a time in the life of Jacob for many years he thought that the son of his love was dead. But Joseph was not dead but the Lord hid Joseph so that his purpose and destiny to help the nation of Israel would come to pass. Something life changing is coming your way soon so don't sell out to the devil.

You must remember that we see in part but God sees all, all the time. This great birthright inheritance of the believer makes you rich just as Jesus the son of God. In the birthright you are a king and you reign in this life by Christ Jesus in you daily. Yes this is what you are in the birthright inheritance. You are a **descendant of the living God** so don't sell out your birth right inheritance like Esau.

King Ahab and Jezebel

King Ahab who lived in the days of the great man of God Elijah. Here is another example of a person who sold out on God just as Adam did. Ahab was born as a prince of Israel and then moved on to become king over the people of God but he had no time for the things of God just like some before him. This man knew that God lived but he planned against God with his wife Jezebel who was one of the most wicked, women who ever walked this earth. Ahab married her from an idol worship background then he forsook the Lord and started out in witchcraft with his wicked wife. He was like many today who go to the house of God read the word of God even sing in choirs but still, will not obey the Lord. The time has come for all of us to repent and really turn back to the Lord. **This world is in very serious problems and is waiting for the manifestation of the sons of the living God.**

Ahab hated the man of God because he did not want to do as God wanted him to do. If he could he would have killed the man of God but he could not because he was afraid of the anointing that was on the man of God. He preferred to work iniquity with his wife over the whole nation than to obey God.

Right in the midst of all this, God sent a man with his word in his mouth that could not be stopped. The same thing is about to happen again there is about to rise up a new generation with the same kind of power anointing that, was on the Prophet Elijah. This new wave of Gods might will, flow through them and the world will wonder where these people are from and will be afraid of them. No sickness or disease will be able to touch them as they speak the eternal word over problems. Just as the world has gone crazy there is about to be one of the greatest anointing that this world will ever see before the return of the Lord Jesus Christ. Ahab wanted the wealth that God gave to the people of God, yes he stole all from the people and kept them with witchcraft but that could not help him or his family in the end. What we sow is what we will reap. Study Galatians 6.

The man sold him self to do evil in the sight of the Lord and so are many of us today we are selling ourselves for the things of this world. The time has come to seek the kingdom of God first. You don't have to be like Ahab, rise up and make a difference in this world with Gods word in your mouth. Stand up against the powers of evil because greater is he that is in you than he that is in the world. 1 John 4:4. The Lord has given us power over all the power of the enemy, use it well and be counted in the army of the Lord. "You are **the descendant** of the living God" therefore you have his DNA in you right now. His DNA in you is his "divine nature" and power. The power you have over Satan is released as you speak the word of God out of your mouth. Proverbs 6:2. *You are taken by the words of your mouth.*

CHAPTER 11

LOOKING DEEPER INTO WHO WE ARE IN CHRIST JESUS

"Deep calleth unto the deep" Psalms 42:7

"Blessed be the God and Father of our Lord Jesus Christ which according to His abundant mercy hath begotten us again unto a lively hope by the resurrection of Jesus Christ from the dead" 2 Peter 1:1-3

"Blessed be the God and Father of our Lord Jesus Christ, who hath blessed us with all spiritual blessings in heavenly places in Christ Jesus" Ephesians 1:3

1 Corinthians 4:13, "we having the same spirit of faith. The very same spirit that was on Christ is in you and with you now. You are a son of God on the inside".

The greatest miracle of the New Testament is the availability of the new birth to those who wants it. This divine new birth gives us new status in Christ. Subsequently all of this is at the expense of Jesus.

This is for those of you who really want to grow up in the Lord. These scriptures are some of the greatest in the New Testament word of God. We are blessed by God because as the father of Jesus Christ he has begotten us in Christ Jesus. To be begotten means to be born. Jesus called it born again in John 3:1-6. He said *"that which is born of the spirit is spirit*". Jesus said also that "ye must be born again." The greatest thing that can happen to a man is to be born again not of the flesh but of the Spirit of God. The only way to be connected to God literally is by being born of his Spirit in your inner man. Every believer is born again of the Holy Spirit.

This new birth is not a natural birth. It is supernatural in its nature, and it takes place in the heart of the believer. You are a **descendant of God** if you are born again. 1 Peter 1:23. You are his offspring in your spirit. You are his candle/floodlight on the earth Proverbs 20:27. The spirit of man is the candle of the Lord. Ok, so for God to be called your father you must be born again. Understand this; if you are not born again you still have the satanic nature inside of you. Only the new birth can change this no man can recreate you only God can do this thing in Christ Jesus. Local churches may not want to teach on this but this is the word of God. Don't let Satan rob you of what Jesus has made available through the things he suffered for us on the cross 2000 years ago. His blood has given us the right to the new birth. This is legal.

Revelation 3:10 we are washed in his blood. We have redemption through his blood. Ephesians 1:7. The greatest thing we have is the new birth. This is why the Holy Spirit lives in us all the time because we are the very temple of God in the earth. God says in Romans 8:16 -17 that we are heirs of God and we are Joint heirs with Christ. This is a most remarkable thing here in the word. These things are real they are not just things we imagine no, they are real in us now.

The word of God calls us a new creature/creation in Christ Jesus. Now the new creation man in Christ is not subject to the failures of the flesh. In the new creation nature is the nature of the father God himself. This new creation man can only be found in the new testament of Jesus Christ. Corinthians 5:17 "If any man be in Christ *he is a new creature* old things are passed away behold all things are become new." We really need to sit down and meditate on this word for at least a year, until it soaks into our very being. This scripture must become a part of our daily confession until we are *very aware* of what we are in the Lord Jesus Christ.

Begotten us again? Yes we were lost and without God in the world after Adam sold us out big time in the Garden. But Jesus came and by his blood and resurrection brought us back into the fold. You are begotten of the living God. Jesus said, "Many sheep I also have which are not of this fold, them I also must bring that there may be one fold, and one shepherd" John 10. "I am the door of the sheep"

You are the called and separated one of the living God in Christ the anointed one and his anointing Rom 1:6. The greatest king in the universe has called you with a holy calling into his kingdom plan. Jeremiah 29:11. "For I know the plans I have for you, saith the Lord." You are so important to God that he was willing to be spat on in his face for you. He was willing to be naked for you

Let us go deeper into this word

"Blessed be the God and father of our Lord Jesus Christ who hath blessed us with all spiritual blessings in heavenly places in Christ Jesus" Ephesians 1:3

This eternal word means we are already empowered by the word of the father in heaven and we are given every blessing that God has to offer. When God blessed us in heavenly places in Christ, he did an all rounder. Yes, we are blessed forever in Christ Jesus the Son of the living God. A man of God stated "The greatest thing that heaven has given to the earth is the blessing of the Lord." Gen 1:28. The blessing is the thing that was working all the time to produce the new birth. The blessing is God in man and on man.

God does not have any thing better to give to man because he has given himself to us in the blessing. This is what you have in you all the time now that you are in the kingdom of this great God. Let me repeat that

the greatest authority on earth is the blessing. And the blessing is on you Psalms 3:8. It is the power of God himself on the earth in man bringing about the plan and will of God for man in this world and the one to come.

Hear me you are not of this wicked world but you are born of God on the inside this is why he blessed you with all blessings, in heavenly places in Christ Ephesians 1:3. He has called you into his marvellous light and made you a son of light. Now you have "Christ in you the hope of glory." Colossians 1:27. Light is your realm.

You are his new creation in this 21st century and you are more than a conqueror, you are the winner all the time in the Lord Jesus 1 Corinthians 15:57. God gives us the victory over satanic forces all the time because of Jesus. The seed of God in you cannot be defeated and this is what we are in him, 1 Peter 1:23. John said "whatsoever is born of God overcomes the world and faith is the victory that over comes the world" 1 John 5:4

You notice the two words Begotten and blessed in the two verses above? When will we truly understand that God has really begotten us out of himself and blessed us in himself? James 1:18 stated "Of his own will, begat he us with the word of truth that we should be a kind of first fruit, of his creation." This is a sister word to 1 Peter 1:23 being born again not of corruptible seed but of incorruptible seed which is the word of God which liveth and abideth for ever. When the word talks about we are the righteousness of God in Christ this is the word that explains how God did it in heaven in the invisible world of spirits.

You see, in the spirit world it is a well known reality that we are the sons of the living God descendants of the, Most High God of Abraham. Now then if we are really of God why settle for the weak things of this world when the divine table in Psalms 23 is laid up for us. Everything you need is already on the divine table, so come. All we need to do is come and dine. Jesus said in Luke 14:17-23 "***Come for all things are***

now ready." The time has come to step into your destiny and fulfil your divine purpose. This destiny is not something that is of man but of God. <u>*"Ye are of God little children and have overcome them because greater is he that is in you than he that is in the world" 1 John4:4.*</u>

Let's go deeper in this word this is not tradition

We came out of God not the world or the devil so we are of God, yes we are the manifested sons of God by revelation faith and knowledge. We are tapping into the wealth of who we are in Christ Jesus. This is it now the enemy can't hold on to what is ours any longer. We refuse to let our blessing leave us. For too long Satan has been stealing from the body of Christ but now the eyes of the church is being opened by the Holy Spirit. This is coming about by the word of faith teaching we have been receiving for many years now. We are learning to deal with the devil with the anointing that is on us. We are taking what is rightfully ours back in the name of the Lord Jesus. *"For as many as are led by the spirit of God they are the sons of God" Romans 8:14. If we are sons then we are his descendants. We are his heirs.*

We are sons of God with authority, and absolute power over, all the power of the enemy. Demons have to respect what we have in us and on us, yes they recognised and, must obey the spiritual God given authority of, the descendants of God in the earth Luke 10:19. *"I give you power over all the power of the enemy."*

We may be walking through the valley of the shadow of death and hell Psalms 23 but we don't have to fear because the Lord is with us all the time and, he will see to it that we are not hurt Luke 10:19. Jesus said, "**nothing shall by any means hurt you.**" In making the new creation like himself in Christ this is the greatest wonder of the ages. There is nothing better for man in the whole universe than the new creation gift of God to man. This thing makes us one with God himself (**he that is joined unto the Lord is one spirit**). Jesus is that gift that gives us back the very life of the great father God. You are of God you are not of this world. But you are of the new world to come. You are **the descendant of the Living God**. This is why we have to live by God's word daily.

Man that was a sinner is united in Christ Jesus with divinity forever with the Lord God, but, God commended his love towards us in that while we were yet sinners Christ died for us yes Christ died for the ungodly Romans 5:3-7.

Oh the wonders of this great father God who loved us in Christ before the world began and therefore he would not give up on us but sent, his only son Jesus the word into this wicked world to redeem us back from the curse of the Torah, Galatians 3:13-14.

He hath made us accepted in the beloved in whom we have redemption through his blood the forgiveness of sins according to the riches of his grace. Ephesians 1:1-7

Now you don't have to worry about who don't want you because you are in the God club, the best club in the universe. You are what God says you are and he says "You are accepted in the beloved Jesus" This is what you have now; you don't have to wait till you get to heaven this is yours right now in this world. "As he is so are you in this world" 1 John 4:17.

To be redeemed is to be bought back and once you redeem something or any one you don't have to do it again Hebrews 9 says we have an eternal redemption. This is all yours now but what are we redeemed from? Poverty sickness, disease and anything that is anti-covenant. You are redeemed from all your sins by the blood of Jesus. "Unto him that loved us and washed us from our sins, in his own blood" Revelation 1:5. "For thou was slain, and hast redeemed us to God by thy blood of every kindred, and tongue, and people, and nation. And hast made us unto our God kings and priests: and we shall reign on the earth." Revelation 5:9-10, you are the descendant of God.

What a word of God, we are in with .Jesus and we are kings and priest of the living God. If we are kings we must learn to talk like kings representing Jesus on the earth. We must always be about the fathers business. Just like Jesus did on the earth. I tell you friend this is a new day for believers on the earth God is about to do some things with the body of Jesus Christ that will let the world wonder and wonder. A great revival is about to take place in this world where many will come to accept Jesus Christ as the Son of the Living God. We are descendants of the Lord God of heaven and we are on kingdom business.

We are the righteousness of God in this world we can't be defeated. For he hath made him to be sin for us, who knew no sin, that we might be made the righteousness of God in him. 2 Corinthians 5:21. Righteousness cannot fail and that is what you are on the inside.

How can the righteousness of God be defeated? This is impossible. Righteousness can't be poor nor can righteousness be broke Jesus was the righteousness of God on the earth that is why Satan could not handle him. Now it is our turn. "The works that I do shall he do also" John 14:12. As sons of God, we have to do the same works that Jesus did in his earth walk. We must learn to reign over the problems of life. Every time any one came to Jesus he knew supernaturally what he should do he knew what the father wanted him to do.

Nothing shall be impossible

This is the key. It may seem hard in the natural but in the spirit it is not hard for in the spirit realms nothing is impossible Matt 17:*20 "No-thing shall be impossible unto you"*. This is the way we need to be thinking Just like how God say's it, nothing is impossible, to him that BELIEVETH. If God said it I believe it that's it, it is over so I agree and believe and confess only what God said to me. As thou hast believed so be it done unto thee. Matt 8:13. There is about to rise a people that will control their circumstances with the word of God in our mouth. The mouth of the believer will now come to the forefront of this battle we are in. No matter what you believe in your heart understand that it will not come to pass until you say it out of your mouth. All of us have power in our tongue but not all of us are using it the right way.

God is 100% committed to the words of your mouth this is a spiritual law that no man can alter because you are in the image and likeness of the living God. *"You shall have what you say" is very real in the realms of the Spirit Mark 11:23.*

The power you have in Christ Luke 10:19.God's word in your mouth is omnipotent just as God is. The very same power method that God use to create the world is the same power he has given to man to rule over all things in this world, Let them rule Gen 1:26. This is in force forever because we are what God says we are and we are to operate how he says not how we feel. *The power is in what he says, that we then say.* This is the secret of great power and Satan knows this so he will try to steal the word from you. This is why we all need to get the word deep into our hearts night and day. Let them not depart from your eyes keep them in the midst of your heart. Proverbs 4:20-23 People do not determine the events of your life. The tongue shapes your future events not people. Descendants of God are awesome people because we have the very same power in us that was in Jesus.

Oh that we would all in the body of Christ just grow up in Christ and take him at his word. The time has come to really grow up in the things of God. We have been in the failure realms for too long. God made us winners not failures so we need to rise up and be counted in the gospel of Jesus Christ. The highway to success is this word of God in the mouth of man. This is the secret that I have been looking for all my saved days and did not understand until some years ago. I had longed for this revelation knowledge but it was already in my hands and I did not know it. *But thank God for men Like Kenneth Copeland and Charles Capps and Fred Price and John Francis and my bishop, Bishop S.E. Grant who mentored me.*

David Oyedepo also help me much and **Matthew Ashimolowo** at KICC in London UK. Most of them don't know it, but their books helped me over the years as I would not give up. Now I can clearly say I am who God says I am no matter what the enemy says, that don't matter my own words are far more important than anything Satan have to say. I live only by what God says to me in his Holy word. Let the word of Christ dwell in you richly Colossians 3:16 Solomon said, "Let them not depart from your eyes." Proverbs 4:20-23 If the word is in you richly, you will have to speak it out, and then as you speak it out, you will see the glory in your life big time. Your words dictate your future all the time. As a descendant of the living God you better make sure you do not for get this reality because if you do, the enemy will use it against you greatly.

The word says we are to "Reign in life by one, Christ Jesus" Roman 5:17 Ok, this mean that we are kings because only kings have the right to reign. God has given us the right to reign on the earth on his behalf. It is the Christ in us that gives us the power and the right to reign. What are we suppose to reign over? Poverty, lack, debt, distress and famine and so on. Basically we are to reign over our circumstances. You are a king so take over now and, command your angels to work for you night and day Hebrews 1:14.

This is done with the words of your mouth. You do not back off but you keep speaking the word of the living God until change manifest. Always remember that it is what you say that will shape your future so don't talk like the world but as a son of The Most High God. You are an ambassador for Christ. You represent the greatest government in the universe. There is no king richer than your king. His riches is yours by the rights of blood covenant!

Never let the enemy reign over your home or your relationships but drive him out of your territory and don't ever let him back in the name of the Lord Jesus (give no place to the devil). **Your time has come** to reign so reign now in the name of Jesus Rom 5:1. You have received abundance of the grace of God, to do this successfully. You are what God says you are in his word not what people say. You are what God almighty says about you and, he has said much about you in his word. Learn to define his word and say it over and over until it becomes a part of you. The enemy will come but be strong in the Lord and in the power of his might Ephesians 6:10. What you have in you puts you over what Satan and his cohorts. They know it but you have to, know who you have in you. Christ in you the hope of glory Col 1:27. *"Give no place to the devil" Ephesians 4:27.*

Praise God all the time for what he has already done within you and walk in the light of the word you already know. Bless the Lord oh my soul and all that is within me bless his Holy name. Psalms 103:1-7.You are the descendant of the living God. You are not of this world but the one to come. You have divine status in Christ Jesus our Lord. This is a most remarkable reality in the spirit realm. We are partakers of Christ we are partakers of the Holy Spirit we are partakers of the Lord's Table. What has really happened is that, the Lord is sharing his own life, with the body of Christ, so his life is now our life, this is why the word says Christ is our life Colossians 3:1-4.Christ is our life. Again Christ is our life.

We are raised with the anointed one out of the failure systems of this world and we have been translated into the kingdom of Christ. We are delivered from the power of darkness and we are now in the kingdom of Christ Jesus. Colossians 1:13-14. When Christ who is our life shall appear we shall appear with him in Glory. Wow, He is coming back for us soon. Looking deeper into who we are will change our life if we look at ourselves from what God say about us in his word. This is a new day for believers because e the coming of the Lord is so near and heaven is really invading this world with the gospel of Jesus Christ. There is a **mighty bussing** of angels in the realms of the invisible and they are here to bring to pass the word of God that we speak out in this hour. **Massive new ministries** are about to be born and much more miracles ministries will burst forth by the power of the Holy Spirit. Joel 2 says it shall come to pass in the last days (I will pour out my Spirit on all flesh).

True prophets of the living God are about to rise up that will take nations by storm. There are Prophets around today but not all are real. However a surge of heavy anointing will saturate the true prophets that those who are false will not be able to stand before them. God told Joshua "No man shall be able to stand before you all the days of your life." Joshua 1:1-8. This is the radical type of anointing that is about to fall on the body of Christ. The prayers of the saints have reached the throne room of the father and God is about to shake the nations far more than what we have seen so far.

Very shortly a new group of believers will rise up to take God at his word and do great exploits with the power of the Lord Jesus Christ on them. I pray you are one of them reading this teaching. There will be a greater understanding of the invisible spirit realm of God and angels, man and demons. Greater healing signs will transpire than we have ever seen before higher levels. These signs will astound the world but the wicked will not give up their sins. The body of Christ will learn to listen to the Holy Spirit. There is coming a time of no lack in the body of Christ all needs will be met supernaturally. We will know that we are his descendants in the earth to fulfil purpose Romans 8:28.

Things in the natural world will get worse and worse but the body of Christ will excel in this new anointing that is here upon on us now. The blessing will put the church on display with the power of the living God. Sickness will run from the body of Christ. The power of God will break out in the local churches. We will all begin to understand who we really are in Christ Jesus our Lord. The Spirit of the Lord is already doing this thing in many local churches around the world. The days of the weak church is over something new and wonderful is about to break out in the body of Jesus Christ. Some of these mighty prophets of Jesus Christ will shut down wicked governments. And institutions that are wicked.

We now carry the very life of Jesus Christ in side of us. This life is actually resurrection life the same life that was in Christ Jesus our Lord. Rom 6 teaches that WE SHOULD NOW WALK IN THE NEWNESS OF THIS LIFE/ZOE. This is what we have and what we are in the Lord. This is why Jesus said the least in the kingdom is far greater than even, John Baptist or any old testament Prophet. Most of us in the body of Christ have not meditated on these things the way the Lord wants us to. But this is the way we will get it to manifest in our daily lives. We cannot help the world when we walk as mere men we have to learn to walk just like Jesus in his earth walk. He that saith he know him, ought himself also to walk even as he walked 1 John 2:2-8.

We are taught in the word not to walk after the flesh but after the Spirit Romans 8:1 in short we are to copy the Lord all of our lives yes we are to mimic him all the time as children do the parents. Be ye therefore followers of God as dear children Ephesians 5:1. This is why we aught to be learning for the rest of our lives how to speak like the Lord all the time. Our work is to speak the language of God.

No wonder the word says we can do all things in Christ who is our supernatural strength and power. With Jesus in us we are winners all the time there is no more room for failure thanks be to God who gives us the victory as a free gift all the time without any limit, 1 Corinthians 15:57 We are descendants of the living God so His power has been give to us by the Holy Spirit. Matt 10:1-2.

Deep is calling unto the deep Psalms 42:7. The Lord is calling the body of Christ out into the deep things of God now. He wants us to learn to walk by faith in the new creation realities of what the Lord has made available to the church. The Holy Spirit is calling us into the deeper things of the word now. Deep is calling you out of the failures of life into the success of Christ Jesus. It is really time to grow up in the Lord now because we are running out of time and people are dying around us.

Now the Lord had said to Abraham Get thee out of thy country and from thy father's house and from thy kindred into a land that I will show thee. And I will bless thee and make thy name great and thou shall be a blessing and in thy seed shall all the nations of the earth be blessed, Gen 12:1-3.

Like Abraham I believe the Lord is calling us out of our comfort zone into the vast blessings he has given us in himself. He wants us to step out into the deepness of his word/promised land by faith as Abraham did many years ago and became the father of faith. Abraham had to move into new territories that was unfamiliar to him and so do we. As we obey God as Abraham did, we will see astounding signs and wonders from the Lord in our lives. Abraham had a messed up background but that did not stop God from calling him into purpose and destiny. Your life may be in a mess right now or maybe you are not where you would love to be in life but this makes you a perfect candidate for God to use in these end times that we are in. Align your life with the word of God and you will rise to the level of miracles.

The time has come to take the power of the Holy Ghost and strike back at hell for all the things Satan has been doing to the church. God wants a Church that will attack the gates of hell itself and take back what is rightfully ours. We can only do this as mature son not as babes in the Lord. Look at the power of the baby church in the days of Peter and understand that today we have far more information in the word.

We can only help our communities when we are reigning in Christ Jesus. Jesus said we are to open their eyes and to turn them from darkness unto the light and from the power of Satan unto God, that they may receive the forgiveness of sins and inheritance in Christ Jesus. We must accept who we are in the Lord for this to take place because flesh and blood cannot stop Satan. We have to be in the spirit to deal with the enemy who is a spirit. Satan is not flesh and blood. We must use the power that God has given to us in his words. *James 4:7 Resist the devil and he will flee from you.* Ephesians 4:27 also say give no place to the devil.

Too often we give in to Satan but this will have to stop now in the name of the Lord Jesus You were chosen in Christ before the foundation of the world according to Ephesians 1:4. Now if this is so which it is, there is no need for us to be worried about any thing because all of our time on earth is already planned out by the father God. All we need to do now is learn to walk and talk like, him which will give him the opportunity to bless us as we do his word as a life style. What the Lord is searching the earth for are a people that will take him at his word all the time. God does nothing in this earth with out first speaking it to his servants/descendant/sons. He is looking to see who will use their faith so he can bless/empower them in this generation.

Spend time in the presence of the Lord daily so that your inner man will be strengthened with the might of the Holy Spirit. Just as your body needs food to live so your spirit need s the word of God to develop and grow up in the things of God. The job of your inner man is to grow the word of God and bring forth fruits. Your inner man is the ground that the word needs to be able to produce what God said to you in this world. You see the word is spirit and you are spirit so when the word stays in you it will supernaturally do the things the word only is able to do.

The word works secretly first of all in the inner man. This is why we must engraft the word into our inner man daily as a life style. This is why Daniel was so effective in Babylon. He and his companion made sure they lived by the words of the Torah that God gave them via Moses the man of God. You have to make a stand and be counted if you want to walk with the Lord in the kingdom power that is available to us. You can't live as a sinner in the midweek and come to church on Sunday and believe all is well the devil is a liar. You will end up in hell if you do not start to do the word of God.

If you trust God and start to do as he says in his word he will help you all the way to the very top. Blessings will over take you as you obey the word of the Lord. Remember who you are you are a new creation in Christ Jesus our Lord. The blessing of the Lord will make you rich in all areas of life but, you must obey his word. Understand that the most important thing to God is his word. All things in the universe depend on the word of God for life. Not even Satan could live if it was not the fact that God lives. We also live because he lives for ever and so will we.

The life that God give to us is given to us in his word, the word is called the word of life or the word of faith. When we have faith in God it is the word we have faith in because we cannot see God but we can see his word so we must train ourselves to agree with God all the time. Most people believe only what they see in this natural word but what you see is not the truth however the word of the Lord endures forever and ever.1 Peter 1:23. This is the same word we preach all the time. Learn to value the word far more than what you see with your eyes. For we walk by faith not by sight.

What ever God says about us is always the whole truth that cannot be altered by anyone in this world. No man can change the word of God to us. The scriptures cannot be broken. John 10:35. It is impossible for God to lie. Gods word is always sure forever. If this is so then, what we need to truly rely on is the word of God that cannot be broken. Not even death could break the word who is Jesus. Hell could not hold him and now he has the keys of death and hell. Revelation 1:18.

Do you remember in the book of Daniel when the king passed a new law that no man should pray for 30 days? Well Daniel broke the law and stayed faith full to God and the word of the king failed because God's word cannot be broken. His word is Power-filled/ miracle filled goodness- filled. Now that word is already in your mouth right now and in it is the very core of the life nature of the Lord God of heaven. The hungry lions could not touch the faith full man of God because he trusted in our invisible father Dan 6.

How can the father, let us down when we put our trust in him at all times. He said "I will never leave thee or forsake thee." No matter what is going on in your life stay faithful to the Lord in all things and he will give you the desires of your heart. Do not lean to the arms of the flesh because you will fail put your full trust in the Lord all the time and seek his kingdom first and he will bless you all the days of your life. You are the descendant of the living God. This is what you are in Christ. You are a son of God himself on the earth.

Let us go deeper

He revealeth the deep and secret things he knows what is in the darkness and the light dwells with him Daniel 2. In Daniel chapter 2 the word declares how Daniel and his partner's lives were suddenly threatened by the enemy. The king had dreamed a dream forgotten the dream but wanted the wise men of Babylon to tell him the dream and also to interpret the dream. This was some thing new this was a hard king to deal with. When Daniel found out what was going on his life was at stake. But he asked for time so he could seek God. God will reveal his secret to them that fear him and take him at his word. Daniel was a faithful man of God. It was not long after that God spoke to Daniel all he wanted to know. There is about to be the outpouring of new revelation faith in the word of God and great new insights into what God is saying in his word. Joel 2.

The body of Christ is about to grow up in maturity in the Lord. This will bring about the greatest demonstration of the power of God that MEN HAVE EVER SEEN IN THIS WORLD FROM SINCE DAYS OF MOSES. The Holy Spirit so anoint men with his fire power just like Jesus that the world will marvel. The power of God will send terror into hell itself, before the return of Jesus, to the earth. This is why the spirit is now teaching the body how to live by faith in Gods word daily. Matthews 4:4. A new generation is rising to take the gospel of Christ to the nations of the world. Greater inventions than the internet is on the way. We have not seen the best in new technology yet. The best is yet to come. The body of Christ is about to astound the world system. Jesus is coming for a full grown church, an Elijah type of church.

New teachers will rise up by the power of the Holy Spirit that will astound the world. Men like Jakes is only the tip of the Iceberg of what God is about to do. Men like Benny is only a small piece of what the Spirit is about to do. Heaven is about to invade the earth. This will be done by the remnant people of God a covenant people on the earth that will not back off from what God say's in his word.

Problems that have been threatening the people of God for years are about to be wiped out by the power of God in the mouth of his people. Waves upon waves of the glory of God will hit the earth. Angels will be seen more than ever before in this divine invasion. Get ready Get ready. We are living in the time of revelation knowledge now so get ready for God to talk clear to you than you could ever imagine. You are his descendant so act like him. The famine is over and the glory is here.

CHAPTER 12

THE DOMINION MANDATE HAS NOT CHANGE IT IS STILL IN FORCE

Genesis 1:26 God said "Let them have dominion and God blessed them, and God said unto them, Be <u>fruit-full, multiply, replenish the earth</u>, and <u>subdue</u> it and <u>have dominion</u> over the fish of the sea, and over the fowl of the air, and over every living thing that moveth upon the earth Genesis 1:28. You have supernatural dominion power over satan himself.

Now friend, God is not like a man who changes his mind daily. Once the Lord has spoken nothing in heaven or earth can change what God has said about us in his word. I want to look now at the mandate of God to man. I want to take a much closer look at Gen 1:28. Here we find the very clear plan and divine mandate God gave to man when he made man. Be fruitful and multiply and replenish subdue and have dominion over the earth we are the descendants of the living God John 1:12 we have been given power to rule and reign over the enemy. 2 Samuels 2:1-3 thou hast enlarge my mouth over mine enemies. God made the mouth of Hanna greater than the bareness that tried to intimidate her for so many years.

May the Lord open your eyes right now in the name of Jesus so that you can really see who you are in the Lord. See that <u>you have dominion</u> power over the enemy right now, Luke 10:19 and Revelation 12:11. All the power that Satan has is not above your tongue. You just need to see in the spirit who you really are in Christ. You have dominion.

The first thing that God did for the man after creation was to bless him with dominion power. The word dominion means, to have power authority control, command, domination, dominance, territory, region, state, kingdom, it also to rule. <u>You are king.</u>

Dominion could not work without the <u>Blessing</u> of the Lord on Adam. The glory and power of the Lord God was place <u>into</u> Adam and <u>upon</u> Adam. God never expected the man to be alone on the earth God's plan was to live in man by his own Spirit that was placed in the man. The dominion that you have is a supernatural dominion; it is the invisible power <u>of God himself on your tongue</u>. There can be no dominion control until you learn to use your tongue right like Jesus. This power of dominion on your tongue is far greater than any thing you can see in the natural world around you. This great power is still available to those of us that will rise up and use it against the enemy. You have to speak out.

You can take it and shut down the problems of life that tries to intimidate you just as Jesus did to the fig tree. That fig tree was a type of the various problems of life that we face in our life time on earth. We all have to learn to shut them down with our tongue. Jesus said we shall have what we say. Mark 11:23. There is no dominion without the use of the tongue you must learn to talk like God all the time.

This secret is all over the bible but we have not embraced it the way we should because of religiousness. Time us now upon us to move away from any self righteousness and just do as the word says as a daily routine. Do not let the devil steal your blessing any longer open your mouth and God will fill it with his word. Satan cannot resist the word of God in your mouth nor can any type of circumstances of this life. No storm is above what YOU HAVE IN YOUR MOUTH. You have dominion power inside your tongue/mouth.

Jesus expected the disciples to shut down the storm but they did not. I command every storm the enemy sends at you, be shut down in the name of the Lord Jesus Christ. Man is the temple of the living God, 1

Corinthians 3. This is why he blessed the man, because man would not be able to function in the things of God without the blessing of the Lord being on the man. So man was endowed with the power of God to take charge of this world. It was a global responsibility that God gave to Adam.

The power that God gave to Adam was totally unlimited over the earth. How was this to work? Adam spoke after God, yes all he had to do was say what God said and as long as he did that all was well. He fell to the enemy when he left the word of God out of his daily routine. He left the word of God out and bowed to Satan his enemy. Now then, we know that the purpose of the enemy is to steal kill and destroy John 10:10. But, Christ came that we might have life and has it more abundantly.

One of the benefits of the blessing is "dominion," this word mean we are to reign over the whole earth. God s plan for man was to have him control all in the earth and man was placed over all of God's creation. The main realm of man was to be the earth where God put the man into the Garden and gave him power over all things, so the man was able to expand the Garden with his dominion power the was given to him by The Lord.

Before the man was created God said let them rule over all the earth and over every thing in it. God did not put an angel over the earth but man which was his own family and we are supposed to run the earth just as how God runs heaven with his word in our mouth. Adam gave Satan dominion over the earth when he sinned against God. This word dominion is a very powerful word to meditate on for a few months.

Adam lost dominion when he fell from the light realms. This man Adam had total control over all and gave it to the enemy of God. Now when Jesus came into the earth and gave his life for us on the cross with his blood, he got back the dominion for all of us. Luke 10:19.

Man needed the blessing in order to be able to walk like God. Without the blessing we can't win we can't help any one. The blessing is the key to success this is why we must operate in line with the words of the blessing. The blessing words are the pattern of the Lord to do any thing that he plans to do in the earth. The man was blessed by the Lord God before he told him to be fruit-full. To be fruit full is to be productive. This is a normal function of the blessing. This is why Abraham was so blessed it was the blessing on his life that made him so rich. It made an old man fruitful in his old age because the blessing does not depend on the natural. The Fruitfulness is what the blessing does all the time.

Now as believers we need to understand that we have this same power in us all the time, 2 Corinthians 4:13. None shall barren among the people of God. It is very important to know that you have dominion over Satan because if you don't he will use things and people to intimidate you in the affairs of life. God expects the body of Christ to act just as Jesus did in his earth walk John 2:8. Jesus said in my name shall they cast out devils they shall lay hands on the sick and they shall recover. To be able to cast out devils mean we have all power over them. This power is what Adam had in him in the garden. The time has come for us to rise up in dominion power and take back all that Satan has stolen from the body of Christ. If we have been given dominion over Satan in the body of Christ why do we let him get away with so much against our family, the church and our loved ones?

I say in the name of Jesus I refuse to give any place to the devil. Proclaim the word over your life daily and with dominion power be fruitful. We have the dominion mandate but if we do not put it to word with the words of our mouth and talk like God this dominion will not work for us. This is what is going on in the body of Christ today. When we aught to be using our mouth to help others we don't, but we use our mouth to pull each other down. This is a very bad thing going on in the body of Christ and the Holy Spirit is about to put a biog stop to it. The body of Christ is going into its supernatural destiny, where no weapon formed against it shall prosper.

Yes Jesus has given us the dominion back but we must use it daily and learn to develop in it greatly. The word says we must grow in grace and in the knowledge of the Lord Jesus Christ. The things of the Lord, is things we have to learn to grow into. The word says we must Grow up in Christ Jesus Ephesians 4. It take time for trees to grow and so it is with the things that God is showing us in his word they are so great that some times it may take us years to really understand the things that the Lord is saying to us at times.

What we need to do is keep on staying in the word daily and we will learn from the Holy Spirit as he unfold the word of God to our inner man. You see, the outer man will never be able to understand the things of God but it is with our recreated spirits that we learn to tap the things of the word of faith. *"Turn you at my reproof behold I will make known my words unto you I will pour out my Spirit upon you" Proverbs 1:23.* "Faith cometh by hearing and hearing by the word of God" Romans 10:17.

If we really want to know God we will have to spend proper time in this word. Most of us these days do not really study the word the way we should, but we are always depending on the Pastor's faith but this will not always work for you because the storms will come and the Pastor may not be able to be there for you. So you better get into the word of God for yourself so you can know the wisdom of God when the storms do come your way. Believe me they will come to you. It is not just a super few in the church that have dominion over the enemy, all of us do who are born again but not all is reigning in life by Jesus Christ Rom 5:17. With dominion power in us we move from the realms of being the victims to the realms of the winners. God don't make losers in him we are all winners all the time.

God said about you "let them rule" Gen 1:26 Jesus said, "see I give you power over all the power of the enemy" Luke 10:19.

Jesus has never changed his mind about his body and we are the body of Christ. Now in the natural we take care of our bodies and so does the Lord take care of his body which is the church. The greatest power house in the earth today is the body of Christ. It may not seem so at the moment but by the word of the Lord I am informing you that we are about to turn the world upside down again with the Power of God upon us. There is a new anointing flowing now and it is only going to increase until the return of the Lord Jesus to take his body out of this wicked and sinful world.

With this new anointing on the descendants of God operating in the new anointing that is coming heaven will be back on the earth again. We are the sons of the living God in the earth with his dominion mandate in us. As soon as they hear you they shall obey you Psalms 18:43. This is talking of those with the power of God working in our lives. There is a new flow of the waves of God coming to us it is here now and will grow daily out of the midst of the body of Christ. Thy blessing is upon thy people Psalms 3:8, the blessing is the power dominion of God on man in the earth.

The woman with the issue of blood was still bleeding but she took the dominion power of God and touches Jesus and was made whole. You can do the same. It is as you do take dominion that you will see the miracle power of God. Remember that just like Jesus you are for signs and miracles and wonders Acts 2:22. When you are tithing you are taking dominion over the enemy, it is not just when you are praising but, it is also when you are giving the way God says you should do it. ***Until you take dominion over your money it will take dominion over you.***

Take dominion over your sickness and drive it out of your body until you are no longer getting sick any more. You will also lay your hands on the sick and they shall recover before your eyes Mark 16:15-20. The word says God working with us confirming his word with signs following. It is so wonderful to know that the creator is working with us. We are the body of Christ we are the sons of the living God 1 John 3:1-3. You are a son of the living God walking the earth today with the glory and power of God in you all the time.

You must never forget this, but daily you need to meditate on the reality of, your divine status in Christ Jesus. You are the **descendant** of God himself. All of this has taken place because Jesus went to the cross for you and paid the price in full with his precious blood. Now we overcome satan by the blood of the Lamb and by the word of our testimony. Rev 12:11. The blood of Christ gives us dominion over satan. The name of Jesus gives us dominion over satan. The word of God gives us full dominion over satan.

The time has come for the body of Christ to accept who we are as descendants of the living God. What God says is what we are no matter how we feel no man can change that. Why let satan control you when God has given you power over all the power of the enemy? The Shunamite son was dead in the Old Testament but she would not permit it and got her son back by the power of God. Many times in life we just give up on what God has for us and we let the devil steal what is ours. Those days are over in the name of Jesus Christ. Take on the attitude of Jesus where he said, (all things are possible to them who believe) Mark 9:23.

Believe what? The word of the living God. This is what we must stand on in our hearts but we will need to open our mouth as well and say only what God says. Believe you have this dominion over satan and use it and God will back you all the way God will always back His word if you will obey and apply it daily as a lifestyle.

Believe in your heart all the time that you are what God says you are in his word. Believe it and say it very often. Do not stray away from what God told you in his word, this is where many are going wrong and they are messing up big time. God's ways of working is by his word and this will never change because God does not change at all. You have been given divine dominion over the earth use it well in the name of the Lord Jesus. The dominion you have in you is the power of the Lord God himself and this power is totally unlimited. You are the descendant of the living God. The modern church has lost the power of God it cannot help the community as the true believer can. The time of failure is over we need to get back to the word of God and work the works of Christ. **We can do all things through Christ who strengthens us by his mighty Spirit Philippians 4:13**. We can now use the power of God to stop the work of the devil. We have what it takes on the inside of us. We have dominion over the power of hell.

Go take new territory with the grace and favour of the Lord on your life. Don't settle for little any more because your God is a big God and he is ready to bless you big time. With dominion power in you, you can go expand the Kingdom of God into the earth. You do this with the gospel of the Kingdom in your mouth daily.

Some thing has happened to me

For many years I have been searching the word of God looking for ways to get miracles from the Lord. In this great search of mine I always knew that God had more for me but I could not seem to put my hands on it. Then around 1991 I found the writings of **Kenneth E Hagin**, this changed my life in terms of the way I think. However I still did not see the signs and wonders that are meant to be in the life of the believer so I kept on praying and searching the word.

One day I came to the writings of Charles Capps, Kenneth and Gloria Copeland, I also heard Pastor Penny Francis say one night at Ruach Ministries that 'God did not put impossible on us when he made us and sent us into the world'. I therefore concluded that it was the work of the devil to hold man down but the work of Christ is to bring man up to the divine level. Then I found the writings of David Oyedepo. These great people helped me much along with my Bishop J A Francis. Now I am seeing the power of God in my life and finances as never before.

My ministry is changing and the Lord is giving me now a global ministry. It was a shock to me when I found out that God wanted me to write books. Now I can see many books in my spirit. I will write at least 30 books before I leave this world.

I have many times walked into a meeting and tested the power of God to see if what I have been meditating on will work and it has big time. I don't tell the people but I make sure I depend on the Lord and do as he say to me and he always back up his word. You are not reading this by accident. Life may not have been nice to you but please do not give up because God is about to turn your life around by his mighty power. The secret is to always say only what God say about you in his word. This was the secret of the Lord Jesus and John the Baptist. They said only what God said about them. This was the secret of King David as well. You have to learn to say of the Lord and if you do this as a lifestyle you will see great power flowing out of you and meeting the needs of others around you.

If you want to see good all the days of your life then you must take the word of God and say them all the time. This will give you dominion over all your enemies. Psalms 18:43 As soon as they hear you they shall obey you. You shall have what you say Mark 11:23 so your tongue puts you in charge of the affairs and the storms of life. Descendant of God is what you are yes you are in the family of the great God of heaven. You have dominion over satan himself. Refuse to let the enemy get any place in your life or family Ephesians 4:27 "Give no place to the devil." Satan did not defeat Adam it was Adam who did not open his mouth against the devil when he was talking to his wife. Genesis 3, he was beside eve and said not a word. Same thing is going on today in the church we wont stand up and be counted in the army of the Lord. We have all these great promises but we don't stand on them like David did and killed Goliath. We have to now stand up and fight for what we know is right.

We all have things we have to face in life we all have storms specially the silent ones but, if we stand on the word all of heaven will stand with us. Jesus stood on what the father told him and not even death could stop him. I see you taking dominion over all your enemies in the name of the Lord Jesus. The word says "rule thou in the midst of your enemies." I see you ruling in Jesus mighty name. Where you fell down in the past you, will never fall there again in the name of Jesus.

God has blessed you with dominion but you have to exercise power in order to see God work for you. You will have to run towards the Goliaths of your life speaking the word of faith. You are who God says you are not what people say. You have the word of faith in your mouth therefore you are in charge not the devil. Not the sickness or the infirmities. You will never be financially down graded again in the name of Jesus. Your money is on the way to you in Jesus Mighty name. Luke 10:19 I give you power over all the power of the enemy.

You have dominion power so use it.

This power and dominion is in and gives you power over the demons of poverty that has been stealing your wealth from you. I decree that from today you will never be broke another day of your life. Once you get this into your spirit and keep it there you can't be broke. Let them not depart from thine eyes Proverbs 4:22-24. All that you need is already in you Acts 1:8. God gave Adam all that he needed in Gen 1:28. All that he needed for life on earth was in those words. This is what we fail to understand. Your authority comes from the second Adam Jesus who whipped the devil and gave you his power to rebuke the devil and take back what is already yours. The word says all things are yours. Plus as a blood covenant person you own the earth and the heaven as well.

It was at the cross that you got your victory so don't forget the cross as many Pastors are doing today but the devil is a liar and the blood of Jesus still prevails over death and hell and the devil. God does not want to rule over anything on the earth He wants you to rule in the name of Jesus this is why he said let them rule Genesis 1:26. He gave us the right to rule and reign over the earth. I hope now that you can see your dominion over the powers of darkness in the name of Jesus. We over come him by the blood of the lamb and by the word of our testimony.

You have the divine right to cast the devil out of your affairs. This is what you have in you this is why satan hates you so much. He knows you can stop him and take over. So let me repeat that dominion is authority power control and dominance. It means to reign over a territory. Let the word of the lord rest on you now. Every place that the soles of your spiritual foot shall tread upon that, have I given thee says the Lord. Rise up and take dominion over all your enemies in the name of the Lord Jesus Christ. You are the descendants of the living God. 1 Peter 1:23. Gen 1:28. The seed that made you is divine if you are born again.

Let's look at our God given dominion from Deuteronomy 28:1-14. Just as in other places in the word of God our dominion mandate is so clear we have to be real stupid or blind to miss it. But we have missed it for years. But thank the Lord, the Holy Spirit is bringing clarity to a lot of things that we did not understand or would not accept as ours. Knowledge is increasing in the body of Christ Jesus.

Here it is. Deuteronomy 28:1-14 study. "And it shall come to pass, if thou will diligently, hearken unto the voice of the Lord, thy God, to observe and to do all His commandments which I command you this day, that the Lord will set thee on high above all nations of the world".

The dominion we have is conditional to our obedience to the word of the Living God. We have to really decide to live all the time by the way of faith. God's word is not only for the emergencies of life it is a way of living it is a way of life. This is why he said we must diligently hearken to the voice of the Lord our God. The voice of the Lord is so powerful that the enemy can't stop us if we hearken and do as God says to us in his word. *James 1:22 "but be ye doers of the word and not hearers only"*. The person that will stand out now in the body of Christ is the one that will agree with God and voice out his word no matter what we see around us daily. This gives the Lord to bring to pass his word into our lives as we stand on his word all the time. Real dominion is doing what God says you can do.

God said the Lord thy God will set thee on high above all nations of the earth. This mean we will live in a realm with God where the troubles of life can't control us as we walk by the faith of the living God. Train yourself to observe daily and say only what God says about your dominion mandate just like Jesus. Jesus spoke of his resurrection before it happened. What he was doing is saying it in order for it to happen just as in Genesis 1. We must say it if we want to see it Mark 11:23. We cannot experience dominion without the power of our own tongue. The power of the tongue coupled with the word of God in our mouth is an awesome thing. Satan is terrified of those of us that know what we have and he has been working over time with his blinding ministry so that the church don't find out who we are. This is why we need to urgently grow up in the word of faith Ephesians 4.

Understand that with God's dominion power in you, you are always above never beneath. You are at the right hand of God in Christ Jesus Ephesians 1. In Christ you are far above all principality and all power. God has called you son yes you are declared son, which means you have power over all the power of your enemies. God himself is our father and our mother according to the word of God. Do you understand what this mean? It mean you have absolute power over satan the defeated because of what Jesus did at the cross you have been declared king over satan. This is why God told you to reign in life by Christ Jesus Romans 5:17.

You can't reign without you have a domain and a throne and you are on the throne with Jesus Ephesians 1:1-20 because you are the body of Christ and you have his dominating miracle power on your tongue yes your tongue puts you in charge not the devil Revelation 12:11. You can't have dominion without power so God has given you power over all devil and over all the power of the enemy but you must know this works by the sounds you produce daily. You see God need to hear you sound out his word and all things in this world are pre-programmed to hear you and obey you. Why is this? Because you are a son of the omnipotent God who is your father and he would not put you in this world without omnipotence in your mouth.

In the spirit realm there is no gender (male or female) you are, the descendant of God. Again just as Jesus was declared the son of God with power so, God has said the same about you and he has given us all the power we need, in the Blessed Holy Spirit. God put you in charge not the devil. The Holy Spirit is all the power we need but understand this power of the Holy Spirit is released all the time by the power in our mouth. This has always been how God released his great power. Someone had to say it before it could come into this world even though it was already a reality in the world of the Spirit. God is saying about you now this is my beloved son hear ye him just as he said about Jesus. For you are the body of Christ. 1 Corinthians 12:27.

Hear ye him

You are the descendant of God and so you must be obeyed when you open your mouth and release the power of God into the problems of Life. Sickness must hear you because God said hear ye him, poverty must hear you devils must hear you and obey.

The storms must hear you and obey because of who you are, and you take dominion and you use the power that is in your tongue. Your tongue makes you a master a dictator of the events of your life. Things can no longer control you because you are just like the wind that no man can control. The wind goes where it wants and so do you for you are no longer under the control of satan.

St John 3:8 Understand that every one that is born of the Spirit is a person with dominion power on the inside that needs to be released by the power of the tongue every one. How can you be impotent if Omnipotence is your father and mother?

I see you rising up in the Lord and you are at last taking dominion over the devil he can no longer control you or anything in your life. Your days of embarrassment are over in Jesus Mighty name. The future must obey you as you speak the word of God to it. The *2nd verse of Deuteronomy 28 says blessings shall come upon thee and over take you.* We will no longer live under the curse we are children of the blessing and the blessings of the blessing will now over take our lives on a daily consistent basis. Satan can no longer steal from us as we take up our dominion mantle of the Lord in this earth.

As we take up the mantle of the Lord Jesus we will be able to do exploit in the name of Jesus. Remember his name can do all that he could do when he was walking on the earth. Now you can take the same name that Peter used in Acts three and you can release THE MIRACLE POWER OF THE LORD to help others. All this can only take place if we hearken, to the voice of the Lord, all the time as a lifestyle.

Deuteronomy.28:8 The Lord shall command the blessing upon thee in thy storehouses. This links with Psalms 3:8 and Psalms 1 "whatsoever we do shall prosper" and also Genesis 12:1-4 "thou shalt be a blessing because I will bless thee." Why is it that we have not been able to take dominion as God's people the way we should? It is because we have not learnt to talk the language of the living God this is because we are still talking the same way as the world does. Now when we talk like the world we shut the blessing off our lives and loved ones but as we return to the word of the Lord and talk like God says all our needs will be met by the power of the Lord. This can only come about if we talk the faith talk all the time just as Jesus had to in His earth walk 2000 years ago. He that saith he abideth in him should, walk even as he walked 1 John 2:8. This is the challenge we are to walk like Jesus.

God has given us in Christ authority and power and dominion over every thing in this world in Christ Jesus. God said hear ye him this is talking about us as well not just Jesus because we are one in him. God does not see you out side of Christ he sees you the way the word says he sees you in Christ. "Ye are of God" this is the way he sees you. Because you are of God all of the elements of this world have to hear you and obey you. This dominion that we have is tied to the words or the sounds of our mouths. The power is released into the earth realms by the sounds we make.

"Death and life are in the power of the tongue". We may not like to hear this because the devil is cunning us but power is on our tongue whether we know it or not it is there and has always been. The new birth is the confirmation of this great omnipotent authority that you carry in your spirit daily. When we study Deuteronomy 28:1-14 you can see that God has given us power over the affairs of this life plus Jesus said I give you power over the enemy. God said let them RULE. Genesis 1:26.

This blessing is also mobile because it is Christ himself upon man with his mighty power. It will work for us in any part of the world that we are in so He said, "go ye into all the world and preach the gospel and these signs shall follow them that believe the word". To be in Christ with this dominion power in the new birth gives us total power over satan himself. Understand that the power on your tongue is far greater than what the devil has. He is a defeated foe. We are established in the earth and the blessing is what will do this thing. It will not be by might nor by the power of man for it is God at work in the believer.

You are declared a son so use your dominion power. Take dominion over pain and sickness poverty, debt and every wickedness that the enemy is bringing against the people of God. Remember you shall have whatever you say. No matter what is going on in the world, right now the law of faith that God set cannot be reversed it is still in force today.

We are plenteous in goods and in the fruits of our body. We are blessed going out and blessed coming in, in the name of Jesus. You are a descendant of the Most High God. So walk and talk like him every day talk big and act big and you will, see the glory of the Lord in your life. You are the descendant of the Living God.

CHAPTER 13

SHUT IT DOWN LIKE JESUS

Mark 11:13-14. And seeing "a fig tree" afar off, he came, if haply he might find any thing there on: and when he came to it, he found nothing but leaves; for the time of figs was not yet. And Jesus answered and said unto it, "No man eats fruit of thee hereafter for ever" and his disciples heard it. Now look at verse 20 "And in the morning as they passed by they saw the fig tree dried up from the roots. And Peter saith unto Him, behold the fig tree which thou cursed is withered away".

Do you think that Jesus did not know that the time of figs was not yet? Yes he did he knew nothing was on the tree but he wanted to show us the power of words His words on our tongue. The fig tree was a real problem, Jesus really hungry and wanted some thing to eat so he uses the opportunity to teach on the power of the word on our tongue. We see Jesus replying to the tree that was trying to intimidate him. Jesus used words to shut it down. That tree was there for many years but with just a few words spoken to it by the Lord it had to die. You can do the same with you circumstances. You have the same spirit of faith in you as a believer *2 Corinthians 4:13 "we having the same spirit of faith as it is written I believed and therefore have I spoken we also believe and speak".*

Here we have the proof again that the word of God in our mouth is far greater than the things we see or feel in this natural world around us. How can one talk to a tree? But Jesus did. We should never let the affairs of this life intimidate us we should learn to tell them what to do Jesus took dominion over the three and told it to die yes he shut it down with the words of his mouth and so can you and I shut down the things that comes into our lives to intimidate us. Don't you dare ever let your circumstances control you shut them down with the word of faith in your mouth. In your life time you will face many kinds of fig trees that will try to stop you from reaching the goals that God has set for you but you must shut them down Just like Jesus did to the fig tree back then. Descendants of God have this kind of power in our tongue. This is what satan is afraid of. The time has come to take our place in the kingdom of God.

The bills in your home are real but they are not the truth. Learn to take the truth and shut them down with the word of God in your mouth. If this can work with a tree in the life of Jesus it will work with your bills. Remember Jesus is your example your pattern and he said it shall obey you Jesus said Luke 17:6. Jesus further went on to say you shall have whatever you say Mark 11:23. He showed us how to operate like him by using the fig tree as an example of how to deal with the things of life that is here to block our way. Use the truth to bring change.

Shut it down whatever it is that wants to lead you astray from the will of God shut it down with Gods word. It may be a sickness, shut it down now. It may be a great debt that you have failed at removing for years, but take the word now, begin to shut it down. It will take time for your manifestation like what happened to Jesus but you have to start the process with the words of your mouth and you must trust God to fix things for you. Friend as your faith grows you can do the same as Jesus did to your problems of life yes, they will have to hear and obey you. Shut it down in the name of Jesus.

For too long the devil has been using our own mouth against us to shut us down. This have to stop now as we embrace the reality of our new status in Christ Jesus. The enemy has blinded God's people for years now but in the name of Jesus I see God opening your eyes to the reality of who we are in the Lord Jesus. We are his blood brothers and we are in a blood sworn oath with God he has promised to bless us and this blessing cannot be reversed by any one so rise up now and take your dominion power and strike down the devil with it. You are the descendant of God so act accordingly and you will see the power of God work for you.

Is your family falling apart? Rise up and shut down what satan is doing, yes you can stop him with the power of God in your voice, take charge and stop the devil. The doctors have given you a report that is very negative? Shut it down with the word of God in your mouth. Jesus said the works that I do shall ye do also, so believe that and shut it down, shut all wicked fig trees out of your home and life and enjoy the good life God planned for you in Christ Jesus.

You are a descendant of the living God

God's word in your mouth is stronger than cancer, blindness or any other satanic sickness or disease that the enemy sends your way or against the members of your family. I was in Canada and was told that my Grandson was sick. Some thing went wrong with his skin. I told the Lord and the sickness that by the time I got home the boy must have new skin and that is what happened to the boy. We shall have what we say. A friend of mine called me and said her daughter was bleeding and the bleeding wont stop. This was after an operation where something went wrong. I said the bleeding is over and it did in the name of Jesus. If words work for Jesus they will work for his body, we are his body in the earth and, as he is now, so are we, in this world with his power and ability at our disposal. Pull your self together and do as the Lord said in his word and, every fig tree problem in your life will have to dry up in the name of the Lord Jesus. Shut it down. Jesus uses his words to shut down all sicknesses and diseases that he faced in his earth walk. He said; "**I will, be thou clean**" and leprosy had to flee from the words of his mouth. The same power is in you as his descendant.

Whatsoever you bind on earth shall be bound in heaven whatsoever we loose on earth shall be loose in heaven Matt 18:18. So we are the ones that will have to operate the promises by the faith of God in our mouth. Faith is released by the words we speak. Fear is released by the words we speak. We keep putting it all back on the Lord but we have to work with the system he set up in his word. God does nothing in this world without his word. It is a word of faith system and I notice that many in the body of Christ have not reach this level yet. The level of speaking the word into all situations we face daily. They are still saying what they see instead of saying what God say in his word about us and our situations of life. This is why so many have died and gone on when they could have lived until they were satisfied.

God said with Long life shall I satisfy thee and show you my salvation, but have we been speaking this? No. However death and life are still in the power of the tongue as God said. And we shall have whatever we say Mark 11:23. This law of faith will still work for any one that will use it daily. God's laws have no respect for any man they will obey us if we learn to act like sons of God descendants of God in the world today. Our mouth will either loose us or trap us; yes words have the ability to ambush us as I have said way back in this book. For this to work you must understand that you have a covenant of Blood with the Almighty God of Heaven and earth and you are his descendant in the earth today. You have been given divine authority to operate Genesis 1:28 and Luke 10:19 over all satanic forces. Within your spirit is superior forces over everything the kingdom of darkness have but you will have to learn to open your mouth and hold to the confession of your faith in God's word consistently, regardless of what you see in the natural realms. You see, it is the word of faith in your mouth that will release the changes you want to see in the natural. However, the changes can't come unless you release it out of your mouth, this is the system and it won't change for no man.

CHAPTER 14

CONFESSIONS TO GROW YOUR FAITH LIFE DAILY

These daily confessions are all based on the written word of God they are designed to help grow your faith daily. Let them become a part of you daily. Use them three times a day plus, you can make your own as well from the word of God. If you do this daily you will see your life turn around for greatness.

Come on let us go into speaking the word aloud every day for the rest of our life.

I am what God says I am. I am a descendant of God. I am a new creation in Christ Jesus I am the body of Christ. The blessing is on me right now. 2 Corinthians 5:17, 1 Corinthians 12:27 Psalms 3:8, Acts 17:29. My voice creates my future. Proverbs 6:2.

I am the man that God is talking about in Psalms 1 whatever I do shall prosper.

No area of my life shall wither any more because the blessing of the Lord is mine.

I rule now over all problems that come against me and Satan himself in the name of Jesus. I am extremely rich Genesis 1:28 and Genesis 13:1-3. I am in the kingdom I can't be broke.

I am fruitful and success full in every area of my life and my life is getting better and better every day in every way. Thy blessing is upon thy people Psalms 3:8, Romans 8:32 and Proverbs 10:22.

I am a son of the living God a descendant of the Most High. Satan cannot stand in my way. Every thing is commanded to obey me in Jesus mighty name. My success depends on the sounds I produce with my tongue. Luke 21:15.

My mouth is far above my enemies so no weapon formed against me shall prosper but what ever I do shall prosper in the name of Jesus. Psalms 1, 1 Sam 2:1. I take my tongue which is connected to the word of God and my spirit and strike down the enemy with the word of my testimony and the Blood of the Lamb. Revelation 12:11, Mark 11:23, John 6:63. My own words are far more important than anything satan has to say 1 Samuels 2:1.

Whatever I say shall come to pass so I say only what God says about me daily.

I am not weak but strong in the Lord and in the power of his might Ephesians 6:10.

I bind satanic powers off my life and family in the name of Jesus. Whatever I bind on the earth is bound in heaven so I bind satan and his cohorts out of my life in the name of Jesus Christ. Matthew 18:18.

God has given me all power over all the power of the enemy.

Satan has no control whatsoever over my life from today. I declare war against hell and the devil I plunder hell and populate heaven with the gospel of Christ Mark 16:15-20, Luke 10:19.

I am one of the manifested sons of the Lord God in the earth today I shall not want and the blessing of the Lord makes me truly rich. Yes I am rich with the unsearchable riches of Christ in me. What is in me created the natural world. Within my spirit is the creative power of faith where nothing is impossible Colossians 1:27.

The power of the Lord is upon me right now yes his blessing is resting like a dove on me. I am for success and wealth in the name of Jesus. Wealth and riches are in my house as in Psalms 112. My mouth puts me in charge over the devil in the name of Jesus. The devil cannot resist my mouth Mark 11:23 Luke 21:15. 1 Samuel 2:1.

God creates the fruits of my lips so I have to be careful daily what I say because it will come to pass just as I say it to be. I am a sub-creator under God almighty in the name of Jesus. I use the word to create what ever I want from my father creator God. Omnipotence is on my tongue right now. Matthews 17:20. Nothing shall be impossible to the voice of faith in my mouth. Isaiah 57:19.

I am rich and wealthy beyond measure because I am in the kingdom of the great King and he takes care of his own all the time. The powers of darkness no longer have any control over my life. I am delivered and translated into the kingdom of the Lord Jesus Christ I am far from satanic oppression Colossians 1:13-14. Isaiah 54:17.

The Lord is increasing me more and more as he did for Abraham he is doing for me. The Abramic blessing of the Lord is on me forever. I am redeemed from the curse of the Law. I am the seed of Abraham so I am blessed right now. In accordance with Gods Holy words in the scriptures - Galatians 3:13-14 and Genesis 12:1-3.

I am special because I am joined unto the Lord I am one with him because he says so and I agree with God and say only what he says about me. He that is joined unto the Lord is one Spirit. 1 Corinthians 6:17.

I am a partaker of the Holy Spirit himself and he lives in me with all his might and power which is available to me right now. By the blood of Jesus I belong to the Holy Spirit. His divine nature is imparted to me. 2 Peter 1:1-4.

I am saved healed and washed in the blood of the Lamb of God. I am redeemed I am forgiven and I am accepted in the beloved. 1 Peter 2:24. Ephesians 1:1-7.

My time of unlimited favour has come and there is no stopping me in Christ Jesus I can do all things through Christ who strengthens me all he time. This is a new day in the body of Christ Jesus. Philippians 4:13. Matthews 17:20.

God is my source I shall not want. The blessing is my shepherd I shall not want. Mercy is my shepherd I shall not want. I step into my Green pastors by the faith of God within me. Psalms 23, God is my shield and he is my light and salvation. Genesis 15:1-3.

The wealth of the wicked is laid up for me. The word of the Lord in my mouth is my real estate. The blessing of the Lord makes me very rich and adds no sorrow to me. I am rich with the blessing on me today Proverbs 10:22. Genesis 13:1-3.

I take back every thing that Satan the enemy has taken from me over the years.

I take cattle silver and gold, in the name of Jesus Christ Matthews 18:18. Genesis13:1-3.

Confess your redemption in Christ 3 times a day.

I am redeemed from the curse of the Law; I am redeemed from Poverty sin sickness death infirmities failure at the edge of my miracles. I am redeemed from poverty lack and all debts. No good thing will, the Lord withhold from those who keep his word and do them. Ephesians 1:7. Galatians 3:13-14 Psalms 23. Psalms 81:11.

I am redeemed from the curse that was on my natural ancestors. No demon has any power over me in the name of Jesus. I have all power over all the power of the enemy Galatians 3:13 Colossians 1:13. Luke 10:19.

The spirit of restoration is upon me right now. The spirit of redemption is on me right now in the name of Jesus. I agree with God I believe his word and I confess his word day and night as a lifestyle. Mark 11:23. Prov 6:2.

When I lay my hands on the sick they recover speedily because of the blessing of the Lord on my life. I have the powerful healing ministry of Jesus in my heart and I am an Ambassador/demonstrator/representative of the word of God. Mark 16:15-20.

Jesus is my Lord not the devil not problems not the circumstances of life. I may be in a hard place now but I am coming out of this in the name of Jesus Philippians 4:13.

Psalms 46:1-4. The river of life is in me now and no man or devil can stop me.

I am what the bible says I am I am where the bible says I am and no man shall be able to stand before me all the days of my life. No demon can stand before me all the days of my life.

In the name of Jesus I cast out any demon Mark 16:15-20.

I am snared by the words sounds of my own mouth so my words can promote me or they can break me. I speak the word of life over my life and family Proverbs 6:2. Mark 11:23. My secret is the blessing the blessing is my secret power Genesis 1:28.

The sun shall not smite me or my family by day or the moon by night nothing in the stars can be use against me in the name of Jesus Christ. The blessing is my protector/shield from the storms that Satan sends against me. Psalms 121 and Isaiah 54:17.

By the stripes of Jesus Christ I am healed of all sickness and all diseases. No sickness has any right in my body. I will never be sick again because I live in the kingdom of the almighty God and he is my health and my redemption in Christ. Matthews 8:17 and Colossians 1:14.

I take by faith my position of divine status in Christ Jesus my Lord and declare that in Christ no devil can stop me from fulfilling my purpose and destiny. I am raised up with Christ I am sitting with him now at the right hand of Omnipotence. Ephesians 2:1-6 Ephesians 1:19-27.

I am free by the blood of Jesus Christ from all poverty and all lack and all debts these devils can no longer control my life in any way. The powers of darkness can no longer control my life. I bind them in the name of Jesus Christ. Colossians1:13-14 Matthews 18:18.

You are rich so sound it out and it will manifest it self.

I call in funds to meet all financial needs in the name of Jesus Christ. Money thou art loosed unto me now in the name of Jesus money cometh to me now in Jesus mighty name. Mark 11:23, Phil 4:19, Isaiah 57:19.<u>Whatever I say is being created by my voice</u>.

Real estate properties of great value come into my hands for kingdom purpose now in Jesus name. My ministry is huge in the name of Jesus, Numbers 14:28.

Cattle silver and gold come into my hands now, lands come into my hands, and mansions come into my hands now, in the name of the Lord Jesus. I am a very wealth person because I am a son of the Most High God in Jesus mighty name. Genesis 13:1-2.

The very same blessing that was on Jesus is on me right now. God said he will never leave me nor forsake me so I refuse to be afraid of the enemy. The Lord is my shepherd and blessing so why should I worry, Psalms 23.

Every part on my body is healed by the stripes of Jesus his blood in on me right now. Satan has no right to touch me for I am the body of Christ. Yes I am born of God so back off all devils in Jesus name. 1 Corinthians 12:27 Mark 11:23.

I am wealthy I am healthy I have the life Of God in me. My life is now heaven on earth every day. My life is getting better and better every day in every way. Mark 11:23. John 6:63.

God has given me a mouth over all sickness and disease. Pain must hear me failure must hear me the future must hear me and the storms of life must hear me in the name of Jesus. There is power in my mouth to stop the enemy in Jesus mighty name, Luke 21:15.

My house is under the umbrella of the Abraham's blessing so we shall never see when drought come our leaves shall never wither in the name of the Lord Jesus. We are the seed of Abraham through Jesus Christ. We are in the kingdom we prosper all the time Gal 3:29.

I am not from down here I am born of the word of God himself I am the workmanship of the living God this is what I am in Jesus mighty name. Ephesians 2:10. 1 Pet 1:23

I am 100% complete in Christ, a new creation born of the omnipotent word of almighty God. Therefore I say boldly I cannot be defeated by any one because the Lord fights my battles for me. As soon as the enemy hear me they must obey me in the mighty name of Jesus Psalms 18.

This is what I am, a new creation in Christ with the might of the Holy Spirit in me always. 2 Corinthians 5:17 and 2 Corinthians 5:21. Acts 1:8.

I am the very righteousness of God on the earth today in the here and now. Jesus is my wisdom redemption and power. No devil can withstand the might of God on my tongue. I reign on the earth in the name of Jesus and the devil cannot stand in my way or stop me in Jesus mighty name 1 Cor 1:30, Rom 5:1 and 2 Cor 5:21.

The abundance of the grace of God is given to me I have favour with God himself because he is my father and I am Joined unto the Lord himself by the rights of Blood covenant. Yes I am a covenant person therefore satan cannot touch me; I stand on God's word every day in Jesus mighty name in Romans 5:17, 1 John 3:1-3 and Genesis 12:1-3.

With the blessing on me now I am empowered to bless others in the name of Jesus. When I show up with the blessing sickness and poverty have to go in Jesus name. Gen 12:1-3, Acts 1:8. Luke 10:19. Matthews 8:13.

My mouth is 100% enlarge over financial down grading therefore, I boldly declare that there shall never be a financial down grading in my life again as long as I am here on the earth. Everything is getting better and better every day for me and my family. 1 Samuel 2:1-2, Revelation 12:11.

Every worthless demon spirit of Belial that has been operating against me from the 2 heavens is destroyed by fire now in the name of the Lord Jesus. My days of worthlessness are over in the name of Jesus. Ephesians 6:10-20.

I bind every strongman demon of oppression that has been harassing my life and family in Jesus mighty name. Matthews 18:18.

I am the very descendant of the living God on this earth in Christ. 1 John 4:4.

I refuse to let my blessing die in the name of the Lord Jesus Christ. But like David I take back all my stuff from the devil in Jesus name, 1 Samuel 30.

The Lord is my light so I refuse to walk in darkness in Jesus mighty name.

Let there be light in every area of my life in Jesus name Psalms 27:1.

I am blessed I am fruitful I am multiplying I am replenishing I am subduing the enemy and I have dominion over every devil in Jesus name Genesis 1:28 Acts 1:8. Luke 10:19.

I am fertile rich wealthy abundant successful productive in the name of Jesus. Genesis 1:28, Proverbs 10:22, Genesis 13:1-3. I am who and what God say I am. The descendant of God.

CHAPTER 15

SCRIPTURES THAT SHOW US WHO WE ARE IN CHRIST JESUS

Get them into your mouth and heart and start speaking them aloud daily

Meditate on them as a lifestyle and glory will hit your life

1 Peter 1:23 <u>Being born again</u> <u>not of</u> <u>corruptible</u> seed but of <u>incorruptible,</u> by the word of God which liveth and abideth forever.

Genesis 1: 26 "And God said; Let us make man in our image, after our likeness: and let them have dominion over the fish of the sea, and over the fowl of the air, and over the cattle, and over all the earth, and over every creeping thing that creepeth upon the earth."

Genesis 1:28 And God blessed them, and God said unto them, "Be fruitfull, multiply, replenish the earth, and subdue it and have dominion over the fish of the sea, and over the fowl of the air, and over every living thing that moveth upon the earth".

2 Corintians5:17 "Therefore if any man is in Christ Jesus he is a new creation, old things are passed away, behold all things are become new".

2 Corinthians 5:21 "For He hath made him to be sin for us who knew no sin, that we might be made the righteousness of God in Him."

St John 1:12 "But as many that have received to them gave he power to become sons of God."

St John 3:1-6, "That which is born of the Spirit, is spirit that which is born of the flesh is flesh."

St John 10:10 "I am come that they might have life and have it more abundantly".

St John 21:20, "As the father hath sent me even so send I you".

St John 17:16, "They are not of the world even as I am not of the world".

St John 15:5 "I am the vine ye are the branches".

1 John 4:4 "Ye are of God little children and have overcome them, because greater is he that is in you than he that is in the world".

1 John 5:4. "Whatsoever is born of God overcomes the world".

1 John 3:1 "Behold what manner of love the father hath bestowed upon us that we should be called the sons of God".

1 John 3:2 "Beloved now are we, the sons of God".

1 John 4:17, "As He is, so are we, in this world".

1 John 5:12 He that hath the son hath life, he that hath not the son of God hath not life.

Romans 2:28 "For he is not a Jew which is one outwardly; neither is that circumcision which is outward in the flesh. But he is a Jew which is one inwardly and that of the heart".

Romans 8:1 "There is therefore now no condemnation to those who are in Christ Jesus who walk not after the flesh but after the Spirit".

Romans 8:13 "For as many as are led by the spirit of God they are the sons of God".

Romans 8:16 "The Spirit Himself beareth witness with our spirits that we are the children of God".

Romans 8:17 "If children, then heirs of God, and joint-heirs with Christ".

1 Corinthians 12:27 "Ye are the body of Christ".

Ephesians 1:3 "Blessed be; the God and father of our Lord Jesus Christ, who hath blessed us with all spiritual blessings, in heavenly places in Christ Jesus".

Galatians 1 4:7 "And because you are sons God hath sent forth the Spirit of his son into our hearts crying Abba father".

Ephesians 2:10 "For we are his workmanship created in Christ Jesus, unto good works which, God ordained before the world began".

Colossians 1:27 "Christ in us is the hope of glory".

Galatians 2:20 "I am crucified with Christ nevertheless I live yet not I but Christ liveth in me, and the life I now live in the flesh, I live by the faith of, the Son of God who loved me, and gave himself for me".

Revelation 5:10 "He has made us unto our God kings and priests and we shall reign on earth".

Acts 17:29 "We are the offspring of God".

Luke 10:19 "Behold I give unto you power over all the power of the enemy to tread upon serpents and scorpions and nothing shall by any means hurt you".

Acts1:8, "Ye shall receive power after the Holy Ghost is come upon you".

Mark 11:23 "Ye shall have whatsoever you say".

Matt 17:20 "Nothing shall be impossible unto you". "As thou hast believed so be it done unto you" Matt 8:13.

Luke 17:6 "It shall obey you".

Mark 9:23 "All things are possible to him that believeth".

Numbers 14:28 "As you have spoken in my ear says the Lord, so will I do unto you".

Proverbs 18:21 "Death and life are in **the power of the tongue**".

Isaiah 57:19 "I create the fruit of the lips". Understand that words create.

When you engraft this word of faith into your heart for about 3 months and speak them daily at least three times daily, you will begin to see God work for you but your role now is to get them into your heart and into your inner man. Do this by speaking them out loud daily. Agree, believe and confess.

Your inner man is designed by God to grow what you put in it so as you keep the word before you day and night you will begin to see the wonders of God because you will be tapping into the powers of the world to come. That world in your heart is all powerful it is the realm where nothing is impossible.

Proverbs 4:20-23 "My son, attend to my words; incline thine ear to my sayings. Let them not depart from thine eyes; keep them in the midst of thine heart. For they are life to those that find them, and health to all flesh. Keep thine heart with all diligence for out of it flow the issues of life".

It will take you time as it has taken me time but you need to just simply live by the word daily in spite of what is going on around you. You see, satan knows you want to get this word into you and if you do his hold over your life will be over so don't give up just do as I am telling you in this book and your life will turn around for the better. Hold fast to the confession of your faith in what God told you in his word because it cannot be reversed by the devil.

Living inside the Kingdom of Christ

Your mouth is over the devil so give the word time to work for you, don't give up keep at it day and night until your faith is built up then daily live this way for the rest of your life. Day and night do the word. The devil can't turn what you say out of your mouth because your mouth is over the devil. Luke 21:15 I will give you a mouth that all your adversaries shall not be able to gainsay nor resist. What the Lord is showing us here is how to live in the kingdom and how to use the power of the kingdom.

Real power is tongue power and this has always been so with God and man but when man fell he lost the knowledge of how to operate in this kingdom power. You see what has been happening is that satan has been taking advantage of this ignorance in man. He has been able to get us to use our own tongue against our own selves. This is so in the invisible and the natural but you have to know it by faith.

We are in a kingdom language war that started in heaven long ago. This started in the third heavens. Read Isa 14 There you will see how satan tried to exalt himself like as if he was God. Jesus came into the world to show us how to operate in the kingdom of God. This we do daily in everything we do with words. God does nothing without words and you are the same. In the beginning was the word and the word was God the same was in the beginning with God all things were made by him and without him was nothing made that was made. St. John 1:1-3. The blessing is on you now so look out for great things to happen to you.

<u>You are the descendant of the Living God himself so act like it</u>. Go and unleash the might of God against the enemies of the kingdom Of God. "There is no restraint to the Lord, to save by many or by few." 1 Sam 14:6. Finally understand that Jesus Christ is Lord.

Now as we draw near to a close in this book 1, I want to show you some final things to help you. According to the word of God you are already in the kingdom of God. You are legally in that realms from the day you were born again in Christ. Actually you were translated in to it by the power of the Holy Spirit based on the word of God that you spoke when you accepted Jesus Christ into your life. Who hath delivered us from the power of darkness and hath translated us into the kingdom of his dear son. Col 1:13-14. Most people in church that are born again do not understand that we are already in the Kingdom of Jesus Christ. <u>You are within his kingdom now you have to see this now by faith</u>.

Where you are you can't be sick. Where you are you can't be broke nor can you hear any evil tidings where you are. You are in the kingdom of Christ. This is what Psalms 112 is talking about. Yes this word is talking about the man that resides in the Kingdom of God all the time. You can also see the same man in Psalms 1 and slams 23 and psalms 91. This is why we need to learn to talk like our omnipotent father all the time. In the kingdom your leaf-life shall not wither and whatever you set your hand to it must prosper because in the kingdom you always have the Blessing on you Psalms 3:8. <u>Thy Blessing is upon thy people</u>.

<u>There is no evil in the kingdom of Christ Jesus and this is where you are now</u>. Who hath delivered us from the power of darkness and hath translated us into the kingdom of his dear son. Col 1:13-14. You don't have to wait for the benefits of the kingdom because, you are in the kingdom. We <u>just need to learn to operate in it just like Jesus did in his earth walk.</u> You physically walk on the earth but in the spirit you are in the kingdom of Christ. Every kingdom citizen has all power over the power of the enemy Luke 10:19. ***Nothing shall by any means hurt you*** because of where you are, and you become conscious of it daily. This is

the secret; to know where you are in the realms of the spirit. The next thing to know is how to speak; and this mean you must always say, only what God says about you, all the time and as you do, you will activate kingdom dominion power, in your life to help others.

Now listen real well. The kingdom is hidden inside of you and it is upon you and around you. You are the visible part of his kingdom on the earth this is why he wants to display his power through you to the nations of the world. Learn daily to live out of the kingdom of God that is in you and it does not come with observation it is all by faith and this you get from the word of God. The word of God is the word of the kingdom. Mark 4. The words of the kingdom are miracle working words and they always come in seed form. They are planted when ever we as men speak. Your mouth has the ability to operate in the kingdom of Christ all the time. It is connected to his kingdom. <u>You are in the kingdom that rules over all</u>. Psalms 103:19.

As a citizen of the kingdom you have the right to command changes to the glory of Christ. You have the right to the blessing of Abraham. You are the descendant of God.

When we learn to live and reside in the kingdom it will be easy to deal defeat to the devil in every encounter. There is no need to be broke or poor or lack because kingdom minded citizens' can't have any lack at all. No poverty is in the kingdom all things are new in the kingdom. Therefore if any man be in Christ he is a new creation all things become new 2 Corinthians 5:17. Living in the kingdom is an urgent necessity that the Holy Spirit is calling the body of Christ into.

Believers who learn to tap kingdom power can't be defeated that is impossible. We cannot be helpful to others until we tap into kingdom power like Jesus. In the kingdom nothing is too hard nothing is impossible. The modern church has not yet learned to walk in kingdom dominion power the way God has planned it to be. This is about to change. Now this is not baby stuff this is hard meat but we have to say these things now. The Lord has been waiting on us far too long now. We must rise into our real status in Christ now.

You are His, and He is yours, period!

Watch this space. . . Book 2 is coming soon

You are the descendant of the Lord God.

This book:

- Opens your eyes to the real you
- Challenges you to speak change
- Will bring you success in all areas

www.ingramcontent.com/pod-product-compliance
Lightning Source LLC
Chambersburg PA
CBHW060355080526
44583CB00012B/316